The Power Law of Information

The Power Law of Information

Life in a Connected World

Srinath Srinivasa

Response Books
A division of Sage Publications
New Delhi • Thousand Oaks • London

Contents

List of Figures

Preface

May you be born in interesting times.

—An old Chinese curse

We live in a world of unparalleled technologies for information processing and communication. Within a matter of a few years, the very framework within which we process information has undergone tremendous changes. Because information is so crucial to our livelihood and, indeed survival, the societal changes that we are now witnessing can have potentially fundamental and far-reaching impact.

Several theories predict a "liberating" effect brought about by information and communication technologies. Inherent in these theories is the understanding that the information age will put an end to hierarchical social systems, liberate both individuals and societies from ignorance and, by implication, repressive policies. Further, it will break down bureaucratic structures and bring transparency in the working of organizations. Not only that, the information age would also create a "global free market" making free trade possible across national borders.

While there are several examples substantiating some of these claims, is this the entire story of the information age? Are we really stepping into an era when all bureaucratic formations disintegrate and society becomes a flexible networked structure? Do organizations become more flexible? Do economies automatically transform into free markets? Does an individual enjoy unfettered freedom with regard to his/her information needs?

There are clear indications to suggest that the answers to these questions are not completely positive. The very technologies that inform and liberate can be used to obfuscate and repress. Technologies that enable citizens to connect to the world can be used by governments to exert even greater control. Technologies that enable a breakdown of organizational hierarchies can actually be used to enforce stricter hierarchical norms. Technologies for communication can be used to track individuals, intrude into private lives, deny service and prevent communication.

Admittedly, not all of these negative consequences may be by design, and not all control is necessarily bad or repressive. A certain level of control is always necessary for maintaining integrity in a social system—like enforcing laws and preventing illegal activity. However, does an information-rich society automatically evolve into one where legitimate flexibility is allowed, while illegitimate ones are not? The objective of this book is to explore this question.

We will see that a recurring theme that we encounter while analysing very large information systems is what is called the "*power law distribution*". In intuitive terms, a power law denotes a system with a very small number of extremely powerful entities and a very large number of entities having very limited power. Here *entities* and *power* mean different things depending on the context. In a sense, the title of this book, *The Power Law of Information* is a pun, reminding us that the dynamics of information are usually all about power. This could be the power to control or influence many things: citizens, employee activities, the stock market, immediate friends or one's own life. Power law is simply another technical name for the well-known Pareto 80-20 law (that is, 80 per cent of the wealth held by 20 per cent of the population).

Power law distributions are characteristically found in what are called "frictionless" non-linear systems. A frictionless system is one where transaction costs are extremely low. Because of this, any event in the system is likely to cause a large number of transactions. Frictionless systems are prone to what are called "non-linearity" in their behaviour. In intuitive terms, this simply means that events and their repercussions are so finely intertwined that it is often impossible to ascertain what is cause and what is effect. Not only do actions cause consequences, the consequences in turn influence the same action further on.

Conventional methods of reasoning about systems fail when applied to frictionless non-linear systems. Several properties of frictionless non-linear systems seem counter-intuitive when compared with conventional wisdom. A sound understanding of these is crucial to formulating policies and making good decisions.

Frictionless does not mean "hassle-free". Just because transaction costs are extremely low does not necessarily mean that all hurdles to achieving objectives are removed. Frictionless simply denotes very low transaction costs, and this coupled with non-linearity ensures that actions, consequences, further actions and their consequences are finely intertwined.

The second aspect of information societies that impact on their dynamics is the overall *connectedness* of the system. Indeed, frictionless communication among people throws fresh light on how information societies are connected. Even when it is theoretically possible for everyone to connect to all others in the world of the Internet at very little or no cost; we do not see such social information networks in practice. Indeed, studying the way information networks are formed helps us understand many things about human behaviour and societies. This book also addresses such connectivity issues in understanding information societies.

The focus of the book is on *"what is"* questions rather than *"how to"* questions. I don't think our understanding of this fascinating field has reached a level of maturity where we can offer cookbook recipes for different problems of information management. On the other hand, knowing some characteristics of the societal "big picture" can help us in formulating policies and in insightfully addressing specific problems. The tone of the book is, thus, narrative rather than prescriptive. There is nothing "good" or "bad" about frictionless systems or power-laws per se.

The target audience of this book includes strategic decision makers, policy formulators, entrepreneurs, market researchers, academicians, students and anyone trying to understand the evolving information society. Although concepts in this book are based upon several technical papers, the narrative is targeted towards the non-technical, but informed reader.

Ideas presented in the book rely heavily on abstracting properties of a given system into a mathematical model and simulating its behaviour using a computer. Indeed, one of the main messages of this book is to use the computer to understand larger societal patterns that we could have hardly imagined otherwise.

However, building models implies some level of idealisation. Idealising in this case means considering only a small set of "core" variables of the system to determine its behaviour. Real life of course, is much more complex and that is what makes it so interesting. Modelling and simulation are still important because they help us in understanding some core principles of the system. The results of simulation would "by and large" be true of the system's behaviour.

Idealisation is necessary for formulating a theory. Theories focus on core properties, thus furthering our understanding. Without a model of the core properties, the system's behaviour would appear arbitrarily complex and intricate.

Finally, here are the acknowledgments. This book wouldn't have been possible without the direct and indirect support of several people. Let me start with Manini Sharma, who was initially planned as a co-author but had to opt out due to work pressures. I remember with gratitude the several discussions and arguments that we had about this topic for more than a year, which is what has brought this book to this shape. Infinite gratitude to Bala Sundara Raman and Ajay Sethi for their critical comments and reviews. Thanks are also due to Ramya, Sanket Patil, Saikat Mukherjee, Ambar Hegde, Siddhartha Reddy, Nikhil Chhaochharia, Aditya Ramana, Shibashis Guha, Mandar Mutalikdesai, Martin Meier, Markus Schaal, Sadagopan, Asoke Talukder, S.S. Prabhu, S.S. Satchidananda, Jayant Haritsa, Balaji Parthasarathy, Kentaro Toyama, Sujit Kumar, Venkatesh Guru Rao and Ashima Goyal. Feedback on drafts and ideas bounced off them on several occasions have formed the fabric of this book. Special thanks are due to Chapal Mehra and Leela

Kirloskar from Response Books who have been gently encouraging me to finish this book.

Last, but certainly not the least, the book is dedicated to my wife Radhika, my parents, my sister and my little niece Nikita. Without them, I am nothing.

Chapter 1

Information and the Power Law

The illiterate of the 21st century will not be those who cannot read and write, but those who cannot learn, unlearn, and relearn.

—Alvin Toffler

The Lakshadweep islands lie about 200–300 km west of the Indian coast of Kerala. Being far from the mainland, this group of islands subsists on fishing, coconut plantation and tourism. Till recently, the distance from mainland India posed a major hurdle, especially in the face of medical emergencies. Due to the lack of specialist medical care and timely advice, several lives were lost annually on illnesses. This could have been easily avoided had they been on the mainland.

Around the year 2002, the Amrita Institute of Medical Sciences (AIMS) based in Kochi, Kerala, and the Indian Space

Research Organization (ISRO) launched a "telemedicine" channel between Kavaratti (the capital of Lakshadweep) and Kochi. Telemedicine enabled two-way audio-visual communication between patients in Kavaratti and experts in Kochi. Advice ranged from routine prescriptions to even guiding doctors through complicated surgery. Several potential medical emergencies were detected at the early stages and cured.

On the other hand is the following instance. In distant Mumbai, a college student receives an e-mail apparently originating from eBay, the popular auction portal. The mail asks the reader, in a grim note, to refurbish his eBay account number along with his contact address and credit card information. The reason given is vague, claiming some misuse of his account and the need for a "security clearance".

Many gullible recipients of such mails routinely enter their contact and credit card details, not realizing that they are victims of a new kind of crime called "phishing". When users click on the "eBay" URL provided in the mail, they are actually taken to some other Web server containing bogus pages looking very similar to eBay pages. The unsuspecting user enters sensitive information, which silently makes its way to the perpetrators of this crime.

1.1 The Information Age

Welcome to the "information age". Stories like the ones above were inconceivable as recently as the 1990s. However, today stories like these are becoming increasingly commonplace. They are impacting on us significantly, at times constructively and, at others, destructively.

At the core of this new "age" is the proliferation of information processing and communication technologies (ICT). Recent advances in ICT have introduced fundamental changes in human behavioural patterns leading to new and unexpected changes in our lifestyles, societies, organizations and economies.

Historically, information was meant solely for human consumption. Information was created by humans and processed by humans. However, today information is both created and consumed by machines in addition to humans. As any other mechanized tool, a machine can generate and process far greater amounts of information than a human being ever could.[1]

Similarly, information storage and exchange historically needed a material *carrier* like paper and books or human beings. However, communication technologies have effectively decoupled information exchange with material interchange. There is no need to transport material goods for transmitting information as information exchange is no longer constrained by the physical factors that govern material exchange. Information exchange can be instantaneous and extremely cheap compared to material interchange. As a result, the amount of information that is generated and consumed in an average social setting has increased by several orders of magnitude.

So how big is this increase? The School of Information Management and Systems (SIMS) at the University of California at Berkeley, USA, recently conducted an experiment to estimate the amount of information generated and exchanged using print and "online" media like the Internet and telephone. In the year 2002, we seem to have generated 5 exabytes of *new* information on magnetic media, print, film and optical storage (see Lyman and Varian 2003). To get the mathematics straight, one exabyte is 10^{18} bytes that is: 1000000000000000000 bytes. This is just the amount of *new* information that is added to an already existing pool.

Similarly, an estimated 18 exabytes of *new* information was exchanged through electronic channels like TV, radio and the Internet in 2002. It is also estimated that the amount of new information that is generated doubles in a period of three years, creating an equivalent of the Moore's law for information processing.

To understand how much one exabyte is, let us try counting up to one exabyte. An average desktop computer can count up to 10,000 in one second, given an application program written in a high-level programming language. If we ask this computer to simply count until one exabyte and do nothing else, it will take 10^{14} seconds, which is easily more than 3 million years!

This growth in information generation, exchange and consumption has been unprecedented in human history. The kind of societal changes that this has brought about has been so comprehensive and so fundamental that there is some consensus that we are stepping into a new "era". An "era" defines a new phase of *civilization* itself, encompassing almost all facets of human life like social structures, organizations, economies and nations. An era is characterized by *qualitative* changes in the way we live, and not simply of quantities. An era affects and changes the mental model or the "paradigm" that governs how humans and societies survive.

Perhaps the most vociferous proponent of this theory is the futurist Alvin Toffler. Toffler calls the information era the "third wave" of civilization (see Toffler 1970, 1980 and 1990).

The "first wave" of civilization began with groups of nomads settling down to cultivate fields and form small tribes or villages for survival. It was by far the longest era spanning almost 2,000 years. A few hundred years ago, society (especially in Europe) underwent a major change with the advent of the industrial age. The build-up to the industrial age itself was slow. It was spread over several centuries and many different factors played a role in setting the stage for industrial activity to flourish. However, once the concept of industrial production and manufacturing took shape, society underwent a comprehensive change leading to the "second wave" of civilization.

"Comprehensive change" meant qualitative changes. Villages and tribal society gave way to cities and urban centres. Large joint families gave way to tiny nuclear families. Small feudal societies ruled by local lords gave way to large nation states and culminated in sophisticated administrative concepts like parliamentary democracy.

At the core of this transformation was the emergence of the *factory*. Factories are formal structures optimized for maximum production at minimum cost. The underlying themes governing factories are *mass production* and *standardization*. Mass production and standardization bring similarities in consumption patterns at a large scale thus reducing cost and introducing what are called "economies of scale".

The organizational structures of factories are meant to optimize manufacturing processes. The most common way in which a factory is organized, is the *hierarchy*. It is based on concepts of division of labour and specialization. A hierarchy is such that the lower levels report to the higher level, and where the lower levels perform more specialized job functions as compared to the higher levels.

The factory had such a fundamental impact on society that society itself started to mimic the factory. In large urban centres, specialization of skills was highlighted and, hence, society had different experts, focussing on specific skills. An example is the medical profession which evolved into a number of sub-specializations like paediatrics, gynaecology and psychology. Another example would be cities, which were divided into small administrative zones and their infra-structures were built from a set of standardized techniques and technologies.

Similarly, education started imitating the production pro-cess. Schools were organized to impart "standardized" knowledge in the form of textbooks. Evaluation patterns were standardized bringing in concepts like board exams, bench-mark tests, certification, syllabi and grades. Education started from general subjects in primary school moving progressively to highly specialized subjects at the senior levels.

Such a civilization developed a few hundred years ago and continues to impact on almost the entire human race. This transformation has been near total in industrialized coun-tries, while non-industrialized countries have seen only parts of their societies being transformed into the factory model, resulting in interesting interactions between the first and the second waves.

Such changes nothwithstanding, computing and com-munication technologies have now started to change things in a fundamental fashion once again. The computer itself is seamlessly rooted in the industrial society. The computer was the "ultimate machine" that can be mass manufactured itself and could in turn be used to describe other mass manufacturing schemes.

However, computers along with communications techno-logy have become the drivers of a completely new societal set up that is far different from the industrial set-up.

We are still in the midst of this "third wave" transition from an industrial society to an information society. Many significant changes during the past few decades have shown that the information society would be fundamentally different from an industrial society. Examples of telemedicine and phishing provided at the beginning of this chapter serve to illustrate the fact that the third wave may contain new and hitherto inconceivable opportunities and threats.

Consider the hierarchical organization of factories that is the hallmark of an industrial society. A hierarchy is the most efficient structure that can impart control from the top and production from the bottom. In a factory, both material and information flow is determined according to the hierarchy. A hierarchy is optimized to bring communicating sub-units closer to one another in order to reduce the cost of communication.

However, with inexpensive communication, physical proximity is no longer a constraining factor and information can flow efficiently across geographical boundaries. As a result, we now see concepts like "Business Process Outsourcing" that were all but inconceivable without today's technology.

In addition to organizational structure, the information age has affected us in many other areas in subtle but fundamental ways. Computers, the Internet, mobile phones, Web cameras, and a variety of other gadgets have changed the way people live, socialize, work and play. In general, we are still far from understanding the complete nature of the third wave. The complete picture would perhaps be apparent only in time to come.

There are, however, a number of recurring patterns that might give us an insight into the future. We explore many such patterns throughout the book.

1.2 Properties of Information

Initially, information was considered analogous to any material commodity. Analytical approaches studying information systems simply substituted information in place of the (material) commodity and proceeded with existing analytical models.

However, it is now clear that information possesses properties that are very different from that of a material artefact. Materials are constrained by the laws of physics, whereas information is not. A piece of information may exist in multiple locations at the same time, whereas a material can only be in one place at any given time. Information is replicated with negligible cost, whereas replicating material is costly.

So what *are* the properties of information? How do we use information? To address these questions, it is important to understand how information behaves within a larger system.

Information is defined and used in various ways. The term "information" could mean a *chunk of data* like the stock price of a company, a *stream of data elements* like a movie on television, or a *system of interacting elements* like application software on your computer. Consequently, the *value* attached to an information artefact depends on how the information is used.

Information as a Consumable

In the most primitive form, information is treated as a consumable. The term "information" can be distinguished from "data" by the fact that information adds something new to our existing body of knowledge. However, once a consumable piece of information is added, the information nugget becomes data once again. The information content of that piece of data is now "consumed".

There are several examples of information being used as a consumable. These include stock prices, news and weather reports. This mode of use of information can be exploited for profit by creating a system that continuously produces new information for consumption. Newspapers and financial portals are examples of businesses that rely upon information being used as a consumable.

The survival of such a business is dependent upon what amount of "consumable information" is present in their data. A television news channel dishing out stale news the entire day is less likely to be popular that the one that can bring the latest and breaking news.

Information as a Reusable Artefact

A contrasting view of information is in the form of a *reusable* artefact. Music, books and technical papers are examples of this kind of use. Here, the information content is not completely consumed by first use. They are useful for repeated usage.

A music CD is likely to be heard several times by the same person; a book is likely to be read more than once, and a technical paper is treated as a handy reference for repeated usage.

Businesses capitalizing on this mode of information use have to address challenges of creating content for repeated use. In many cases, the reusability of a piece of information is a measure of the *quality* of the information artefact. A good, melodious song is likely to be heard several times by the consumer, as opposed to a badly sung song. A good technical paper is likely to be reused more than a mediocre one. Businesses capitalizing on the reusability of an information artefact often go to great lengths to assess the quality of such information.

Reusability of information is exploited in business models that charge users per use. Information reusability is capitalized by requiring consumers to *subscribe* to the source of information. A movie theatre is a good example. No matter how many times you have seen your favourite movie at the theatre, you will need to pay again if you want to see it once more. A subscription ensures revenues for every use of the information artefact.

However, the above mode of information use also faces problems of unfettered replication. Replicating information is extremely cheap compared to the cost of *generating* a piece of information. When the value of information sustains over repeated usage, there is an incentive for users to replicate the information at their end for further usage. This property of information can manifest in the form of piracy and unauthorized copying of movies, music, books and other kinds of reusable information.

Unfettered replication is also responsible for the failure of several economic models to accurately explain and predict information dynamics. Conventional economics is based on the notion of *scarcity* of resources. Information artefacts depreciate in value much faster than material artefacts due to unfettered replication. Unfettered replication creates problems of plenty, rapidly bringing down the value of information. At times, the creator of a reusable information artefact imposes an *artificial scarcity* in order to sustain a given value for that piece of information.

Information as a Service

A third view of information is that of *service*. A service entails taking the user through a certain process in order to achieve a given set of objectives. A service is reusable; however, we can contrast it from the previous view of information by noting that it is not the information itself that is reused, but the *service* provided by it. Software is a good example of information as a service: a software package that enables a computer to connect to the Internet is reusable.

One way to distinguish reusable service from reusable information is that every service instance is different. Every time a piece of information is used for a particular service (like connecting to the Internet) it has to potentially contend with new external conditions and challenges. In contrast, no matter how many times one listens to a song on CD, it is the same song.

When a piece of information is used as a service, a measure of its quality depends on how comprehensively it has anticipated external conditions and is able to negotiate them. A software package that crashes when faced with a new situation is likely to be less popular than one that is robust and works even in the face of uncertain external conditions. Reusable information like music or a book, in contrast, is reusable mainly for its contents and is not dependent on external conditions.

Unfettered replication of reusable services are usually handled by embedding sophisticated logic into the service that can determine, for every instance of use, whether it is authorized or not. Based on this, service may be permitted or denied.

Information as a Control Device

Perhaps, the most potent form of information use is as a mechanism for *controlling* or at least *influencing* an external system by selectively releasing or withholding information.

Information is used as a control device in several areas, ranging from social settings like administration to purely engineering applications like controlling an aircraft. In social settings, information is increasingly recognized as a source of "power", much like weaponry or wealth is. Information helps its holder exert his/her influence on others regardless of the others' consent.

Banks, supermarkets, insurance companies, firms manufacturing consumer goods and other businesses routinely collect information about their customers in order to increase their share of the market. Similarly, most organizations gather information about their employees for exerting greater control on their processes, and so do governments about people to influence public opinion and maintain law and order.

Information as a source of power has certain unique characteristics. While it is possible to deprive a person of his/her money and weapons, it is not possible to take away internalized information like knowledge and wisdom from them.

Once a piece of information is given out, the sender in most cases loses control over it completely. Information can be replicated with little or no cost and the originator of the information cannot always control this replication. During the times when carriers of information (such as individuals and print media) were few, controlling the spread of information was easier. However, once a piece of information is let out on the Internet, the sender usually loses control over it.

Information as a source of power and influence would determine some of the major conflicts of the information age as opposed to information as a utilitarian entity. This is the primary backdrop in which this book is written.

1.3 Non-linear "Frictionless" Systems

It may be simplistic to say that a holder of information has the power to influence and control the system: the story of information and power is much more complex. While the holder of a piece of information may selectively release it to influence the system, the fact is the person loses control of it as soon as it is released. The piece of information that the person released may, in turn, feed someone else's body of information, who in turn, may selectively release it in a different context. Indeed, a piece of information released to exert greater control over a system can easily work in reverse and actually serve to limit the influence.

Essentially, information and control are dependent on how the *overall system* is configured. And the configuration of the overall system usually is not a result of design but a cumulative effect of individual decisions. So, how *are* information systems generally organized in human societies? Let us begin our journey into this question.

For describing characteristics of any system, a commonly used method is to describe the *distribution* of one or more entities of interest. For instance, Figure 1.1 is a real-life data set showing the distribution of marks obtained by a class of students in a core subject.[2] The graph plots the number of students obtaining marks in every decade boundary (0–9, 10–19, 20–29, etc.) of the marks. The distribution approximates a characteristic ideal called the "Gaussian" distribution. The Gaussian distribution is so commonly found that it is also called the "normal" distribution.

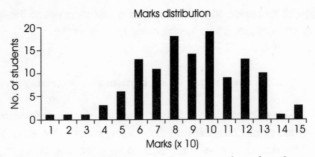

FIGURE 1.1 A real-life data set plotting number of students for every decade of marks obtained in a core subject

In a normal distribution, data points cluster (or form a mound around) the mean or the average value. The average value is also more or less the most frequently found value in the data set. In this case, the average is approximately 83 out of 150. The marks of most of the students lie around the average with a very small number of students having scored drastically above average or drastically below average.

Figure 1.2 shows the ideal curve for normal distribution. The figure plots deviation values from an average value against the *probability* of finding a value with that deviation. The curve is also called the "bell" curve due to its shape. The bell curve and a related discrete approximation called the "binomial" distribution have proven to be very suitable for describing properties of many real-life systems.

What the normal distribution says is that the *expected* value of the marks of any randomly chosen student from the class is very likely to be close to the mean value. Hence, if the mean value of one class of students is higher than the mean value of another class on the same exam, one can safely state that choosing any student at random from the former

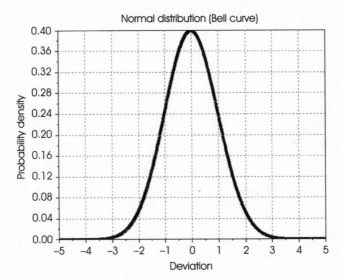

FIGURE 1.2   The "Bell" curve

class is better than choosing a random student from the latter.

Now consider the graph shown in Figure 1.3, which is again obtained from a real-life data set. The figure plots the number of people who have received e-mails from me, against the number of mails I have sent out over several years (about six years).

Figure 1.4 plots the same distribution using what is called a *log-log scale*. In a log scale, every equidistant element is separated by its neighbours by a multiplicative factor, rather than an additive factor. Hence, the first notch on the y-axis depicts 10, while the next notch depicts 100 (10 × 10) and not 20 (10 + 10). A log-log scale serves to clear the large cluttering of data points at the bottom of the graph. The

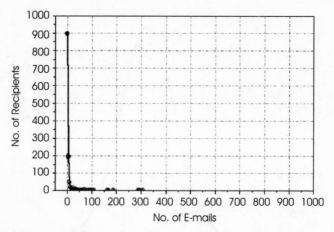

FIGURE 1.3   The number of people receiving e-mails versus
the number of e-mails sent by the author

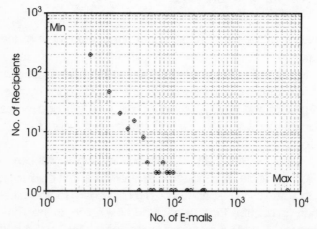

FIGURE 1.4   The number of e-mails sent versus the number of
recipients shown on a log scale

graph starts looking like a straight line with a large base, when plotted on a log-log scale.

Figure 1.4 also marks the minimum and maximum values in the graph. As is apparent from the figure, a large number of people (close to 900) have received just one e-mail, while a very small number of people (1 to be exact) have received a very large number of e-mails (a few thousands) over the last few years.

The average number of e-mails sent by the author is somewhere around 1,500 per person, even though a majority of the recipients have received just one e-mail. This high number comes from the fact that a small number of recipients have indeed received a very large number of e-mails. However, we would be terribly wrong if we were to assert, as in the earlier case, that if we chose an e-mail recipient at random, the number of e-mails a person would have received would be around 1,500. The average value of e-mails per person is by no means the most frequently occurring value among the data points. In statistical terms, the *mode* of the number of e-mails received is very different from the *mean*.

It is apparent that the latter distribution cannot be approximated to a "normal" curve. It seems to be an "abnormal" system of extremes, leading us to believe that the sender of these e-mails shows an "abnormal" behaviour. However, I can definitely assure you that I am perfectly normal, and the distribution of e-mails sent by anyone over a sufficiently large period would have a similar distribution, no matter who the person is! Do try it out yourself.

The distribution of e-mails approximates to what is called the "power law" distribution. To put it mathematically, the power law distribution says that the probability of the random variable (in this case, the number of e-mails received by a person) having a certain value is inversely proportional to some power of a value that is greater than 1. It is written as: $P[X=k] \propto x^k$. But let us not worry about mathematical formulations. I refer to them just for the sake of giving a broader picture.

Intuitively, the power law depicts a situation where a very small number of entities have a very high value of something, whereas a large number of entities have a very small value for the same thing. The power law is also shown to be equivalent to two other well-known distributions—the Pareto and the Zipf distributions (see Adamic 2000).

The main question now is: why does the e-mail distribution look so different from the normal distribution? Is the e-mail example simply an aberration that is to be ignored, or is it indicative of a different class of systems?

Consider the case of marks obtained by students. We can easily see that each point in the graph represents an *independent* behavioural feature. Each point denotes a different student who took the exam and earned a score independent of all other students. This is schematically shown in Figure 1.5(a).

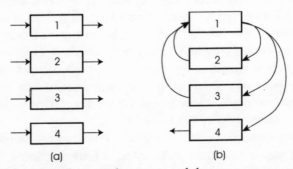

FIGURE 1.5 Schematic descriptions of the exam system and the e-mail conversation system

Figure 1.5(b) depicts the e-mail system. In contrast to the examination system, many e-mails are actually part of a conversation. When a sender initiates a conversation, the recipient responds. This in turn may prompt the sender to further the conversation with another e-mail and more until the conversation reaches a logical end. Of course, conversations can also be group-based, involving several participants. However, the essential property of a conversation, in which responses stimulate more responses, remains the same.

E-mails recorded in the graph are thus not independent of one another. A long-winding conversation between the sender and a given recipient contributes to several e-mail counts for that recipient. Intuitively, it is apparent that a person is likely to have long-winded conversations with only a few persons. Most of his/her conversations would be short, involving a simple exchange of information. And we already can see the picture of a power law distribution emerging.

Conversational systems may be classified as "non-linear" systems, as their mathematical descriptions involve non-linear differential equations in contrast to linear differential equations involved in the former class of systems. Again, we shall not be worrying too much about mathematical definitions.

A characteristic feature of non-linear systems is "feedback". A stimulus provided by an entity in the system initiates a response from the environment or other entities, which in turn may provoke a counter-response by the entity, and so on. This system of response and counter-response can lead to extremely complex behaviours. Since their mathematical descriptions are in the form of non-linear differential equations, most of it cannot be solved by analytical means.

When designing a new system, or analyzing an existing system, the systems are usually treated as linear systems. For example, when designing an aircraft wing it is assumed that there is an infinite stretch of empty space in the front and rear of the wing. The "head wind" in front is assumed independent of the "tail wind" at the rear. Aircraft engines contribute turbulent wakes to the tail wind. If an aircraft flies close behind another, the tail wind from the one in the front becomes the head wind for the one behind, and it can be so powerful as to cause it to crash.

It is not that non-linearity has not been dealt with in conventional systems at all. Non-linear feedback mechanisms are an essential part of engineering systems such as aircraft autopilots, automatic gain control in radio receivers, control of the read-write head in the hard disks of computer systems and control systems in chemical plants.

However, in the conventional systems non-linearity is "damped". The amount of information in the feedback is reduced to a form such that its effect will serve to make only small changes in the system's behaviour and maintain the system's stability. An "un-damped" non-linear system, in which the feedback is not curtailed, is very unstable and is known to generally go out of control.

In contrast, many information networks in social settings are not only non-linear, but also un-damped. In fact, in many cases, social information systems are *frictionless* systems where feedback from the environment is practically total and has the largest possible impact on the sender.

Frictionless non-linear systems are extremely hard to model analytically. The behaviours of such systems are unpredictable and appear to be random, even though theoretically they do not have any source of randomness within them.

Recent research in areas such as meteorology, fluid dynamics, social sciences, economics, computer science and pure mathematics has addressed non-linear systems and shown interesting results. Such studies are usually clubbed under "chaos" theory.

Although far from being comprehensive, chaos theory reveals several interesting properties of non-linear systems. Many of these properties have been defined and explained with analogies that help us understand the phenomenon. Chaos theory and another interdisciplinary field of study called the "theory of networks" provide valuable insights into the way information acts in social settings. Simply put, the theory of networks is the study of *connectivity*. Configurations showing how disparate elements of a system are connected are crucial in determining the repercussions of events occurring in the system.

In the next chapters, we shall visit some of the major results from studies of both chaos theory and the theory of networks and apply them to our concern of information flows in social contexts.

Notes

1. By "processing information" I simply mean mechanical tasks like storing, retrieving, searching, indexing, sorting, etc. I am of course, not talking about processing information for obtaining knowledge and wisdom.
2. Mathematically speaking, the graph shows the *density* function and not the *distribution*. But, we will be abusing this terminology and not delve into the differences between density and distribution functions.

Chapter 2

Non-linear Frictionless Systems

*Every successful organization contains the seeds
of its own destruction.*

—Andy Grove

A commonly occurring pattern in international relations is often seen as variants of the following example: Two mutually hostile countries formulate defence policies based on the mistrust they have towards each other. At the height of their animosity, there is a minor row in one of the villages on the border. The row may not have anything to do with the national concerns as such, but it so happens that villagers of one side hurl abuses against those across the border. Soon the situation gets out of control and the issue assumes national proportions. Government officials of the two countries snarl at each other and the media on both sides relentlessly cover the crisis. Within a few days, xenophobic riots break out in both countries. And it gets only worse and worse.

There are several other such examples where a small issue quickly takes on vast proportions. In such cases, it becomes very difficult to locate the root cause and often to separate cause from effect.

Another good example is of "opinion polls" that are conducted before an election. Are such polls neutral? Or do they actually mould public opinion? These questions are not very different from such questions as, "Are we what we are because of our culture? Or is our culture what it is because of what we are?"

2.1 Thinking in Circles

Information networks are usually non-linear frictionless networks. Consider the simplest case of an information network: a face-to-face conversation between two people.

A conversation involves at least two independent parties and a shared subject. Each party contributes something to the subject and takes the conversation in a specific direction. Whenever one party speaks something, there is usually a response from the other.

The way a conversation goes is governed by the sequence of responses and counter-responses. Especially in informal settings where there are very few rules or norms, it is very difficult to predict where a particular conversation will end up. One might start a conversation by talking about his or her plans for the next day, then go on to talk about places to visit in the city, which may lead to talk on weather conditions, the monsoon, global weather, industrialization, pollution, and so on.

The complexity of a conversation increases when more people join it. Group discussion is much harder to manage than a conversation between two persons. Things get worse when everyone in the group wants to speak to everyone else separately, as part of the conversation. Managing a conference of a group of say, six people is far simpler than managing 15 pair-wise phone conversations among six people. (I'll leave it to you to verify that the maximum number of pair-wise conversations among six people is 15.)

We shall address the question of groups and connectivity in later chapters. Presently the pertinent questions are: Why are conversations so hard to predict? Or, how do we begin to understand conversations?

A conversation involves at least two entities or actors. A stimulus provided by one elicits a response from the other, which in turn invites a counter-response from the first, and so it goes on.

FIGURE 2.1   An influence diagram for a simple 2-actor conversation

Figure 2.1 schematically depicts a simple 2-actor conversation. The arrows in the diagram show which actor influences which actor with stimuli and responses. Such diagrams are called "influence diagrams". Influence diagrams visually depict entities and events of a system and show how they influence one another. They are increasingly used as a tool for modelling and strategic decision making. There are a number of software products that support modelling and simulating systems based on influence diagrams.

The general form of an influence diagram is a "directed graph" comprising entities or "nodes" and directed edges or arcs between them. Each node represents some computation that is performed based on all the inputs coming from the incoming arcs. The output of the computation would flow out on all the outgoing arcs. The computation performed at a node in transforming the inputs to an output may itself be arbitrarily complex.

The influence diagram of Figure 2.1 is extremely simple, but it serves to illustrate the basic idea behind thinking about non-linear systems. As is evident in the figure, a conversation involves a *circular* influence. A circular influence depicts a feedback mechanism where the output from one part of the system comes back as part of its input later on.

A circular influence is the most basic building block of a non-linear system. Each circular influence has its own characteristics; however, we can discern two basic forms of circular influences. These are called the *balancing loop* and the *reinforcing loop*.

Consider a case when the conversation in question is between a parent and one of his/her bored teenage sons who would rather be somewhere else than take part in this conversation. Quite likely, the most common responses by the teenager are monosyllables like "yes", "no", "hmm" and so on. Eventually the parent loses interest or gives up in frustration and the conversation stops. If this does not happen, the teenager grabs the first opportunity to find an excuse and leave, thus ending the conversation. In system theoretic terms, the stimulus provided by one conversationalist is failing to elicit a response from the other, or the response is severely "damped". The stimulus can be seen as a force to move the system state in a specific direction, while damping reduces the effect of this force. Such a circular influence constitutes a "balancing" loop. The push provided by the stimulus is balanced by the lack of enthusiasm in the response.

On the other hand, when both conversationalists are enthusiastic and interested in the conversation, each response adds to the enthusiasm (or "force") of the stimulus. The conversation feeds onto itself and goes on for a long time. In addition, each response is unlikely to push the conversation in exactly the same direction as the stimulus. Small changes in the direction of the conversation accumulate over time and the overall trajectory of the conversation across topics becomes very complex. Such circular influences that build upon one another constitute "reinforcing" loops.

The primary cause of complexity in information systems is reinforcing loops. Balancing loops either die down or stabilize to some point. But predicting how reinforcing loops change the system state or how to manage a reinforcing loop and move it in certain desired directions is a big challenge.

2.2 Sensitivity to Initial Conditions

Consider the influence diagram of Figure 2.2 that depicts competition between two service providers of mobile telephones. The diagram shows how different events in the business affect one another. In this diagram, actors are implicit, and what are more important are the events themselves. This is an influence diagram all the same, as in the previous example. Events represent computational entities in this diagram, rather than actors.

There are two competing service providers and both are investing heavily into advertising in order to lure customers. Almost everyone has some opinion or the other about the two providers and new customers are confused as to which provider to opt for. A perception of which service provider is better than the other determines the service provider that a customer initially opts for. This event is highlighted in bold in the centre of the diagram, depicting the differential preference that a user has for one service provider over another.

If a customer chooses A over B, A scores a small victory over B. The more the number of people opting for a given service provider, the more popular it becomes and the more will it be able to spend on advertising and other media campaigns to increase its perceived value among consumers. A winning spree for a service provider feeds onto itself thus propelling the company forward.

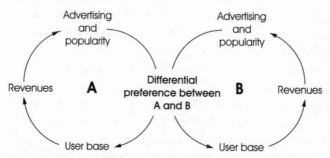

FIGURE 2.2   This influence diagram shows sensitivity to initial conditions. The initial choice between A and B by a critical set of early adopters may seal the fate of one of the service providers.

There is however, more to this story. The growth of one loop is *at the cost of the other*. If users buy the services of A, they have effectively shut off B and vice versa. The more A succeeds, the more B suffers and vice versa.

Which loop eventually prevails depends upon the initial decisions taken by a crucial set of people in choosing between A and B. The central nature of this event is highlighted in bold in Figure 2.2. Small changes in this crucial set of decisions may tilt the balance in favour of one and against the other. Once the balance is tilted, the differences tend to accentuate, since the loops feed onto themselves, tilting the balance further.

This set of crucial initial decisions need not be informed and sensible or based on any concepts of rationality or fair play. In fact, the crucial set of people deciding the larger fate of the system may not even be aware of their crucial role. They may or may not be large stakeholders in the company or biggest consumers.

Malcolm Gladwell, in his famous book *The Tipping Point* (see Gladwell 2000) has used a term, "Law of the Few", to explain the central role unwittingly played by a few people in causing large-scale changes in the system.

In chaos theory, such situations are called "sensitivity to initial conditions". Small changes in initial conditions of the system can make the system go in vastly different trajectories. If at some point of time we notice that the difference in market shares of A and B is marginal, it would be naïve to extrapolate this difference and conclude that the resulting market shares would be largely similar over the years.

Many systems in real life show sensitivity to initial conditions: the weather, for example. Our climate has many circular influences, so much so that long-range weather prediction for specific geographic areas is considered impossible even with most sophisticated super-computers.

Sensitivity to initial conditions is known as "butterfly effect" in meteorology. The weather is supposed to be so sensitive that a butterfly flapping its wings in one part of the world can potentially cause a chain reaction leading to thunderstorms in another part of the world.

Sensitivity to initial conditions arises due to two aspects: a set of reinforcing loops and a principle of exclusion among the reinforcing loops. Reinforcing loops are necessary to pull the system in some direction. However, this by itself will not make the system sensitive to initial conditions. The different ways in which the system is pulled is determined by exclusion properties across the reinforcing loops. If loop A prospers, then B suffers, and vice versa. Figure 2.2 shows only two loops, but most real-life systems have several loops and the sensitivity is far more complex.

2.3 Bifurcations

Consider again the system shown in Figure 2.2. Even when we say that there are only two players in the system, it is unlikely that when one prospers, it is necessarily the death knell for the other. In the real world, we often see competing players surviving or even flourishing by catering to the same population at the same time.

There are at least two factors which we have not really considered in the previous example. The first is the fact that a set of users who are with service provider B would be unlikely to shift to service provider A just because A is more popular. This is because changing service providers means changing the phone number, which in turn entails all the associated hassles of informing friends, relatives and colleagues about the change. Because of this *friction* associated with changing service providers, customers who have chosen B are likely to stay with him, even when A prospers.

The other factor is that neither of the service providers have infinite resources. A service provider who becomes too popular starts suffering from saturation of resources. Eventually user complaints and frustrations pile up, and the popularity of the service provider goes down.

As a result, even though one of the service providers becomes vastly popular, other service providers continue to exist; and occasionally, one could even witness a change in user loyalty, though it would be rare, considering the associated hassles.

Consider now a technology that provides the option of having custom phone numbers for users. A user can "buy" a phone number; and retain the same number for the rest of his/her life, across different telephones, service providers, cities, and even across countries. Such an idea is not far-fetched; in fact, at the time of this writing, there are efforts to introduce such schemes in some parts of the world.

What such a scheme would do is remove the first impediment. It becomes far easier for users to switch loyalties if this switch involves no hassles. The system is frictionless as far as customer loyalties are concerned. The main impediment now would be saturation.

Suppose service provider A prospers initially at the expense of B. The prosperity feeds onto itself and very soon, A attracts such a large number of consumers that its infrastructure starts creaking. Phone calls are dropped, user complaints are not handled in time, accounting mistakes pile up, and a host of other things eventually increase user frustration.

Now, given the fact that it is very easy for a user to switch service providers, a large number of users do change their loyalties.

From A's perspective, this entire process can be seen as a change in the "births" and "deaths" of its consumer population. The analogy to population dynamics is not entirely accurate, but it serves our purpose. When A is prospering, it can be seen as growth in the population of A's consumers, and when it is losing consumers, it constitutes a decline in their population.

The population of any species grows because of an abundance of resources, or at least, a *perception* of abundance of resources. However, when saturation sets in and there are not enough resources for the entire population, the population starts to decline.

When A's infrastructure starts creaking under heavy load, B's infrastructure starts looking attractive. The increase in the attrition rate of A's consumers would then correlate with an increase in the birth rate of B's consumers. However, eventually the same story unfolds with B and there is bound to be further change in loyalties. So, will this story of attrition and loyalties ever settle down?

The analogy with population dynamics gives us a means of simulating this process mathematically. A commonly used analytic means for studying population dynamics is called the *population equation* or the *logistic equation*, which can be summarized as follows:

$$X_{k+1} = rX_k (1 - X_k)$$

Here, x_k stands for the population in the time interval k and the term "1" denotes the maximum possible population that the system can support. In our case, the "1" denotes the total number of people that the service providers are addressing. The population of A's customers itself is shown as a fraction of the maximum population. As before, don't worry too much about the equation. It is given only for the sake of completeness.

The population equation simply states that the population in the next time interval $(k+1)$ is dependent on three factors: the population in the previous time interval (k), a "growth rate" denoted by r and an "incentive to grow" denoted by $(1 - x)$. The growth rate is a factor of the effectiveness of the advertising campaigns and the population's openness to change. The incentive to grow is a factor of how much more space is available for growth. When the population is small, and the system can accommodate much more, there is a higher incentive for growth. When the population is reaching the limits of the system's endurance, infrastructure starts creaking and the incentive comes down.

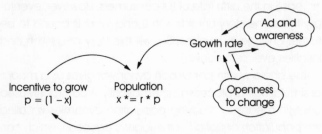

FIGURE 2.3 A schematic influence diagram for the population equation

Figure 2.3 shows a schematic influence diagram for the population equation. The equation has only one circular influence where the population in one time interval influences the incentive to grow for the next time interval. This in turn influences the population. It has r as an input. For our purpose here, we have considered r to be a constant parameter. But this growth rate itself may be determined by how successful the advertising and awareness campaigns were, and how open is the population towards your idea.

We will discuss later on, how to estimate the value of r for different populations. For now, we can intuitively understand that a small value of r denotes a population that is resistant to new ideas or a not-so-successful advertisement/awareness campaign or both. Similarly, a high value for r would denote an enthusiastic population (high on adrenalin, and always seeking out a better life) or a vastly successful advertisement/awareness campaign or both.

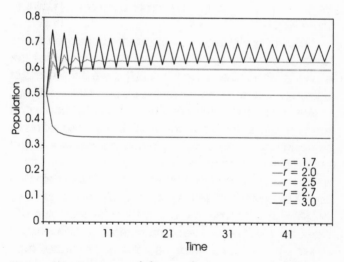

FIGURE 2.4 Dynamics of the population curve with different values of the growth/attrition rate

It is evident that the dynamics of customer population is dependent upon r. Figure 2.4 plots this relationship and depicts simulation runs where an initial population of 0.5

was taken. This means that service provider A was filled to 50 per cent of its capacity.

For different values of r, the figure plots how A's population changes over time. It is evident from Figure 2.4 that when r is small, the population eventually settles down to some value. This is true when the value of r was 1.5, 2.0, 2.5 and 2.7.

Initially, some frustrated customers defect from A and join B's network. However, if this continues, eventually B's infrastructure saturates. Some part of the population now leave B's network and join A. This goes on for a while. However, because of their reluctance to change, this process of defection stops, and the consumer base settles down to some value.

The lower the value of r, the quicker the population seems to settle down to some equilibrium. As r increases (for example, when r is equal to 2.5 or 2.7), there is some kind of a turbulent phase in the beginning before stability sets in.

Now, look at the case when r was set to 3. The population seems to be continuously oscillating between two extremes by going upwards for a while and coming downwards, and going up again and so on. At any given point of time, there is some percentage of the population that is either defecting from A or joining it. While this turbulence seems to be slowly decreasing over time, it is evident that as the value of r increases, the dynamics become increasingly turbulent.[1] Let us see what happens when the value of r increases even further.

Figure 2.5 plots A's population for increasing values of r. As we saw before, when r was 3, at any given time, there is a small percentage of the population either joining or leaving A. As r increases, the percentage of the impatient lot also increases. However, such rise in number does not go on forever.

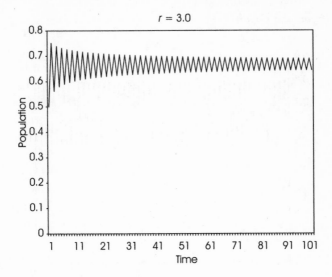

$r = 3.0$

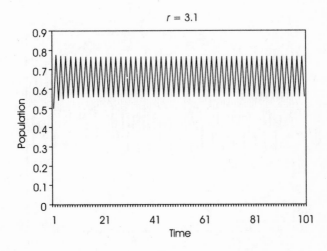

$r = 3.1$

(Figure 2.5 Contd)

(*Figure 2.5 Contd*)

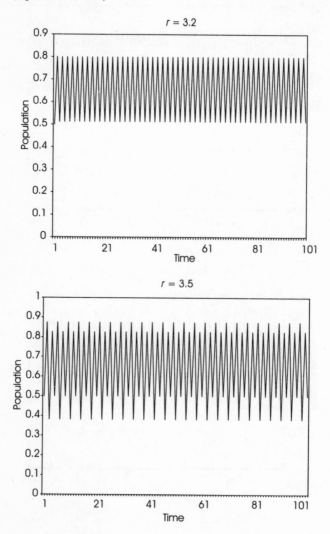

(*Figure 2.5 Contd*)

(*Figure 2.5 Contd*)

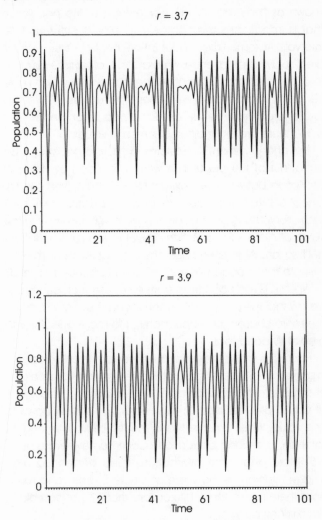

FIGURE 2.5   Dynamics of the population for growth rates greater than 3. Row-wise from top: $r = 3.0$, $r = 3.1$, $r = 3.2$, $r = 3.5$, $r = 3.7$, $r = 3.9$

Beyond a point, for example, when r is 3.5, we see what is known as "bifurcation". The percentage of the population that is impatient seems to be split across different time intervals. At some time, about 30 per cent of A's consumers are displaying impatience, while at some other time it is close to 50 per cent. This bifurcation keeps setting in much more frequently as r is increased further. When r was 3.5 we saw four different extreme values for the population and when r is 3.7, there are eight different extreme values.

This phenomenon is also termed "period doubling". The behaviour of the population when r is 3 can be seen as oscillation between two extremities within a given period. Once a bifurcation occurs, each oscillation has sub-oscillations taking up the same period. With increase in the value of r, the sub-oscillations develop sub-sub-oscillations and so on. At large values, the behaviour becomes so intricate that it becomes very difficult to discern any trend.

When a given population starts exhibiting such behaviour, we say that the population dynamics has become *chaotic*. The more chaotic the population is, the more difficult it is to predict its behaviour.

Figure 2.6 shows the entire phenomenon in one diagram. It plots the different values that the population took up eventually for increasing values of r. As is seen in the figure, at values of r less than 3, the population settled down to one value. When r was set to 3, the first bifurcation occurs. Later on, a second bifurcation occurs somewhere around 3.5. More and more bifurcations keep appearing after smaller intervals as the value of r increases. Beyond some point there are so many bifurcations that it is not possible to discern any pattern.

When the value of r reaches or exceeds 4, the population leaves the specified bounds between 0 and 1 and takes on

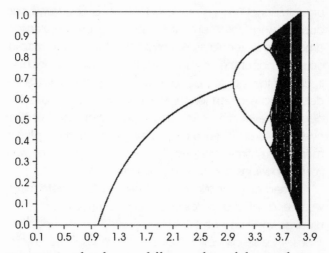

FIGURE 2.6 Plot showing different values of the population for increasing values of *r*

values more than 1 or less than 0. This denotes a breakdown of the system. If we were to be modelling a physical system like an aircraft, this would denote the tipping point where the aircraft goes completely out of control. For our service provider example, this would denote a breakdown of the service provider's infrastructure either due to excessive load or a complete exodus of consumers.

Real-world systems are worse. The population equation with its simple influence diagram of Figure 2.3 is only an approximation. Real-world influences are far more complex.

However, no matter how complex the influences are, reinforcing loops are prone to behaviours that lead to bifurcations and chaos, if the feedback is increased.

Recognizing bifurcations can be crucial in order to recognize the onset of instability. For instance, whenever a new organizational norm is proposed (or say, a new law is introduced by government), it is bound to create debates among the stakeholders. We would hear two or more differing opinions about the new law, either supporting or opposing it. Usually though, the debates eventually die down. Some debates take much longer to die down. But occasionally, debates never die down, and in fact strengthen enough over time to bring grave crisis to the organization or government. Many times, seemingly innocuous banter takes on vast proportions and creates crisis situations.

An idea of bifurcations would be helpful in determining whether a set of debates could lead to chaos and system breakdown. Even if we don't have any idea of the underlying issues, if we simply notice that debates in response to some policy is failing to abate, and seems to be oscillating with the for and against camps becoming more vociferous by turn, and the oscillations seem to be developing sub-oscillations, we had better watch out!

With today's computers one can dream of several new kinds of tools to help us in this. There are many text analysis programs that one can train to reasonably analyse blogs, discussion groups and letters to editors of daily newspapers and classify them according to different topical issues. If we program it to watch discussion groups, Web logs and daily news feeds from the newspapers' Web sites, maybe it can warn us about impending crises!

However, a question that we still have not answered is, how do we decide what is the measure of r for a given population? What does it mean for the value of r to be 3?

Roughly speaking, when r is equal to 3 it means that whenever a person decides to join or leave a service provider, on an average, it leads to two others making the same decision.

Given this interpretation, we can easily arrive at a good enough number for the growth rate by looking at data about users joining or leaving the network.

Behavioural bifurcations have been seen in many real-world data such as weather patterns, river flooding, stock market indices and commodity prices (see, Mayer 2005 for examples). It is likely to be even more prevalent in present-day information networks due to the effortless nature of information creation and exchange.

2.4 Self-similarity

The third interesting characteristic of non-linear frictionless systems is of "scale invariance" or "self-similarity". The idea of self-similarity pertains to how smaller parts of a system share the overall characteristics of the system.

Figure 2.7 plots a set of real-life data. This is the set of daily highs from the Dow Jones index for a period of about 18 years from 1985 to 2003.[2]

Figures 2.8(a), (b) and (c) plot incremental variations in the index between consecutive days. Figure 2.8(a) shows incremental variations in the index between consecutive days for the entire period. Most of the variations are small, but occasionally there are spikes both in the positive and negative directions.

Figures 2.8(b) and (c) show two snippets taken from the plot of incremental variations. Even though both are taken from different parts of the original graph, the similarity between them is striking. There is one large spike, which is preceded by a couple of fairly large spikes. Then, after a period of relative calm there is again a spike.

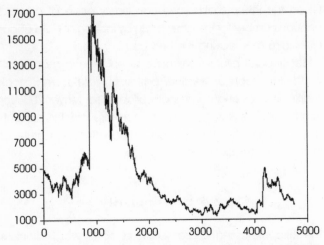

FIGURE 2.7 The Dow Jones Index Daily Highs for 1985–2003

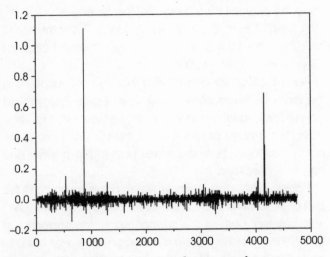

FIGURE 2.8(a) Plot of incremental variations between consecutive days

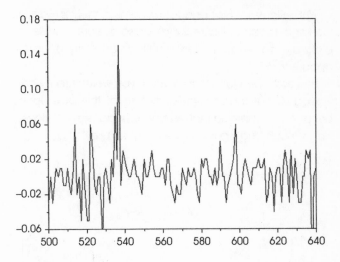

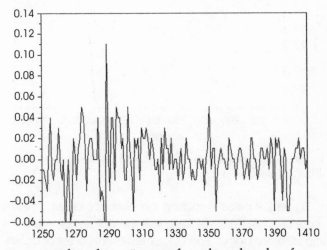

Figure 2.8 (b) and (c)   Snippets from the earlier plot of
incremental variations. The first is between days 500 and 640
and the second is between days 1,250 and 1,410.

While Figures 2.8(b) and (c) are similar, their similarity to the larger graph of Figure 2.8(a) is also apparent. While the plots are not exactly identical, their similarity is visually apparent.

However, I wouldn't blame you if you weren't really convinced about the self-similar nature of the Dow Jones' behaviour. Something that visually appears "similar" doesn't tell us much and would not be of much use.

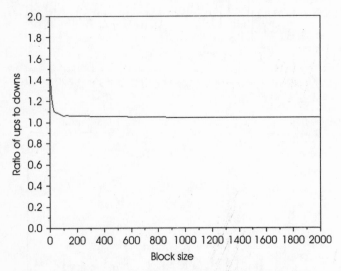

FIGURE 2.9 **Average ratio of number of ups to downs for different block sizes**

Figure 2.9 helps in making the concept of self-similarity more precise. Here, we have split the dataset of Figure 2.8 into different blocks. Each block represents a set of consecutive days. We then counted the number of times the index went up during this period and the number of times it went down. We then took the ratio of ups and downs for each block and computed the average ratio for the entire dataset and plotted it in Figure 2.9.

It is striking to see that no matter what block granularity we consider, the average ratio of ups and downs is more or less constant! Whether you look at this dataset week-wise, fortnightly, monthly, yearly or any arbitrary block of consecutive days, the ratio of ups to downs seems to be the same, hovering around 1.1. In fact, even when we take the entire dataset as one block, the ratio of ups to downs is almost the same. Of course, the value is slightly higher (about 1.4) when block sizes were small (4 days to a block). But given the fact that this ratio can take *any* arbitrary value, the difference between 1.1 and 1.4 is very small, indeed. At no granularity level for example, the index has consistently had twice or three times as many ups as it had downs. Similarly, at no granularity level has the average number of ups been lesser than the average number of downs.

The overall behaviour of Dow Jones in terms of incremental variations over 18 years has the same average characteristic incremental behaviour, no matter at what granularity it is seen from.

There is a famous story of the mathematician Benoit Mandelbrot discovering self-similarity in the behaviour of cotton prices over a period of about 30 years. The prices varied wildly and it was impossible to fit the distribution of prices into any well-known distributions at that time. However, when analysed at different levels of granularity, the cotton prices showed remarkable self-similarity. Its pattern of changes remained the same whether analysed across weeks, months or years. And this self-similar nature of the cotton prices had prevailed across two world wars and the great economic depression of the 1930s.

The same is true for the Dow Jones data set. The self-similar ratio of incremental variations has persisted over a period spanning the dot-com boom and bust as well as the economic repercussions of 11 September 2001.

Mandelbrot's work was inspired by the work of the mathematician Harold Hurst who at the turn of the twentieth century had earned himself the title of "Abu Nile" or "Father Nile" for his pioneering work on predicting flooding patterns of the river Nile. The Nile River seemed to be flooding in erratic ways with extremes of floods and droughts. For centuries, several people had tried predicting the behaviour of the Nile and failed. Hurst studied discharge patterns from the Nile and several other rivers and lakes around the world and observed that flood or drought patterns tend to display similarities across different granularity levels. He then worked out a mechanism to find the constant across scales and a formula based on this constant to predict flooding behaviour. Mandelbrot called this constant of self-similarity "H factor" in honour of Hurst (see Mandelbrot and Hudson 2004; Mayer 2005).

Figure 2.10 depicts self-similarity in the population curve from Figure 2.6. This snippet shows the different values that the population has settled in for values of r between 3.54 and 3.59. The similarity of this set of bifurcations to the overall curve is striking.

Similarity across scales implies that the system (its structure or behaviour) looks as having similar (but not necessarily identical) characteristics when seen on almost any scale. A small part of the system seems to display the same kind of characteristics as the larger system itself.

Why does such behaviour occur? Consider the differences between a system like a stock market and a conventional engineering system such as an automobile. An automobile

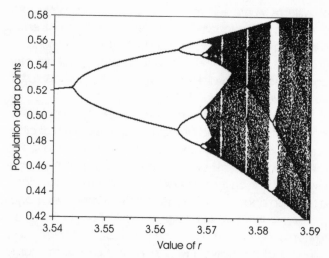

Figure 2.10 A snippet from the population curve in Figure 2.6

is made up of parts whose behaviours *complement* one another in making up the automobile. Every part of the automobile has a precisely defined role. No part of the automobile can be said to be *competing* with other parts. On the other hand, a stock market index comprises several *independent* players competing with one another. There are several reinforcing and saturation criteria in the system at different levels of granularity. There are sensitive conditions that make some part of the system choose and fall into one of several loops at different points of time, leading to behavioural bifurcations. Each bifurcation causes some characteristics of the overall larger behaviour to repeat at smaller scales at faster rates, leading to self-similarity across scales.

While the stock market index shows self-similar characteristics in its behaviour across time, there are other examples of systems where self-similarity in structure has developed due to several autonomous decisions taken in the system. A prime example is the World Wide Web. The World Wide Web comprises of a large number of documents that are inter-connected via hyperlinks. The hyperlink structure displays a remarkable level of self-similarity.

Studies about the Web (see for example: Albert et al. 1999, Broeder et al. 2000 and Elmacioglu and Lee 2005) at differ-ent levels of granularity ranging from a few thousand to 200 million pages have shown that Web pages display a power law distribution on the number of their incoming links. That is, a few Web pages have a large number of other Web pages pointing to them, while a large number of pages have very few other pages pointing to them. In fact, the similarity is so striking that the power law exponent is almost the same (about 2.5) for all these different granularities. This level of self-similarity is remarkable, considering the fact that the Web is made up of pages that were created by several people independently, perhaps without even knowledge of the existence of the others.

Self-similarity helps us in studying a system at different granularity levels using the same set of characteristics. Note that the common feature here is the *characteristics* and not the *values* of individual variables. For instance, returning to our mobile service provider example, we may not be able to predict what would be the exact number of cus-tomers joining service provider A in the next quarter. However, we can chart the behavioural characteristics of the users over the next *several* quarters and predict things like whether the user base is ever going to settle down, or if it fluctuates, in what band would it fluctuate.

In non-linear systems, predicting the specifics is always hard, but it is possible to predict general trends. While it may be possible to predict that there would be "very heavy" rains in Mumbai over the next month, it is very hard to predict how many millimetres would it rain on a particular day in a particular locality of Mumbai.

Notes

1. See Li and Yorke 1975, for an influential paper on this phenomenon of the onset of chaos in non-linear systems.
2. This data is publicly available from Statlib http://www.lib.stat.cmu.edu/datasets/. Last accessed on 8 February 2006.

Chapter 3

Information and Rationality

*It is not ignorance, but ignorance about ignorance,
which is the real problem.*

—Anonymous

It was the days before mobile telephones when making telephone calls was considered a luxury. I knew of a couple
whose workplaces were quite near one another, but who
used to face a curious problem very frequently. They had
just one two-wheeler between themselves. The husband
drove the scooter and left the wife in her office every day
before moving on. In the evenings, the wife waited on the
road for the husband to pick her up.

However, sometimes the husband was delayed at work.
Having no means of communication, the wife waited for a

long time and finally took a rickshaw to the nearest bus terminus and caught a bus home. The latter option was definitely far more inconvenient and expensive than going home by scooter. The longer the wife waited, the harder it became for her to get a bus, and it would be extremely late by the time she reached home.

After this happened a couple of times, the wife drastically shortened her waiting time and started for the bus terminus even if the husband was late by five minutes. On the husband's part, not all of his delays were due to work; sometimes he would be late because of traffic. Whenever it became apparent to him that his wife would not wait longer, it made better sense for him to look for her at the bus terminus rather than at her usual waiting place.

As you might have imagined, there were several instances when the husband, sensing that he would be late, decides to drive straight to the bus terminus. The wife on her part would actually be waiting at the usual waiting place. By the time the husband realised that she might be waiting at her usual waiting place and decides to go back there, it would have become too late. The net result is that both reached home much later than if they had not waited for one another.

There is one more story about electioneering in the days before television and the Internet. Political parties around the world often used a clever ploy to sabotage fair elections and fracture electoral verdict. On the day before the elections, leaflets would be circulated, which mentioned some half-truths that put the most popular opposing candidate in an unflattering light. The timing and the scale of this misinformation campaign were crucial. It had to be done just before the election day, leaving no time for his opponent to discuss it and devise a strategy to counter it.

3.1 Rational Choice and Ignorance

Rationality is the universal form of human behaviour that is common across cultures and geographical boundaries and is predictable and reliable. Most daily activities of people are governed by rational decisions and choices. To be sure, factors such as prejudice, dogmas and delusions also govern human actions. However, over time, rationality has emerged as the single most reliable mechanism in human trans-actions. Business decisions and institutional norms, rules and regulations are formulated with the anticipation of rational behaviour from the people whom it affects.

It is apparent from the two stories given above that inform-ation forms a crucial part of rational decision making. The entire crisis in the first story was due to lack of information, which could have been easily solved with the use of today's technologies such as mobile phones. The crisis in the second story is also due to information; in this case though, misinform-ation or half-truth gave itself so much importance in the minds of the decision makers that it effectively changed the reasoning process.

Rationality is the ability of the human mind to perform activities like inference, drawing conclusions, building models, obtaining knowledge and understanding the world. The process of reasoning is based on a set of facts, observ-ations and assumptions. Rationality has been a subject of curiosity for a long time. In Europe, the "age of reason" is seen as being primarily responsible for bringing its society out of the dark, feudal ages.

There are several schools of thought, which treat rationality as the primary differentiating factor between humans and animals, and as the primary source of human knowledge (see Markie 2004 for a treatise on the debate between Rationalism and Empiricism).

In economics, the term *rational choice* is used to mean rational decisions taken by actors of a system that *optimize* some value(s) of interest. Optimization can mean different things like maximizing benefit, minimizing cost, and so on, depending on the context. Rational choice depends on a number of factors. These include facts, assumptions, rules of inference, and a definition of the "goodness" of a particular conclusion.

Human societies are made of up several rational actors, the actions of whom are not entirely independent of one another. The decisions of one actor may affect the decisions of others, whether this influence was by design or accident. Similarly, the measure of goodness may have different meanings depending on whether it is applied to a single actor or the collective ensemble.

For instance, a person could unilaterally decide that the best mode of commuting to work would be his car. However, his decision to drive to work affects the decisions of others handling the same problem, and who use the same roads. Every actor comes to a decision of driving, based on what is locally optimal, but this may not be globally optimal in terms of road usage. The roads may become overused and clogged because of a number of such individual decisions.

The decision of each individual to drive to work may be based on a number of factors, such as the price of petrol, and the distance to office, as well as a number of *assumptions* such as the amount of traffic on the roads and the time taken to reach office.

Information about facts is essential to reduce our reliance on assumptions. Assumptions are usually made when relevant facts are not available. If everyone who makes a decision to drive to work knew about the individual decisions of all others using the same road, perhaps their own decision would be different. Indeed, it is common to see that someone who decides to drive to work by taking a specific road may eventually discover that "everybody else had the same, bright idea", and the road is clogged every day. He might then discover a new route to work that has slightly bad roads, but far lesser traffic. Of course, as is immediately apparent now, everyone else may discover the new route more or less simultaneously. And so, the cycle goes on.

What is important for us is the role that information and the lack of it play in the process of rational choice. Had each person who makes a decision to drive to work by a specific road knew all the pertinent facts and knew exactly what others who work nearby are also thinking, perhaps, the decisions would have been vastly different.

In the following sections we will see in much greater detail, how information affects rational choice.

3.2 Information-related Fallacies

Human reasoning is far from perfect. Factors such as prejudice, dogma and delusions routinely affect rational decision making. In addition, the ability to reason correctly is itself prone to several fallacies.

For many people, it usually takes a few seconds before the fallacy in the following argument is apparent: *All fish swim, I too swim, therefore, I am a fish.*

The argument is clearly wrong, unless you are willing to believe that a fish can write a book! The statement looks enticingly valid if it were not for its obvious absurdity. The fallacy in the argument is that while all fish swim, not every creature that swims need be a fish.

It is amazing that several such fallacious arguments are routinely made and accepted publicly without questioning. There was an instance where an advertisement of a leading economic magazine showed a child touching a cactus leaf and crying out, "The Truth Hurts". The implication was that if the content in the magazine hurt the established notions of someone, it is just too bad, since "the truth hurts". The advertisement apparently came in response to the magazine being banned in some countries because of its unflattering coverage. However, the argument provided by the advertisement is fallacious. The truth may hurt, but just because something hurts, it need not be true.

There are a number of such fallacies, which are commonly seen to distort reasoning. Fallacies are so commonplace that many of them are given labels like ad hominem, circular reasoning, burden of proof, false dilemma, appeal to authority, and so on.

While many of the fallacies are due to incorrect inference processes, some of the fallacies can be traced to *information*—either the availability or lack of information.

The first story narrates fallacious (or at least sub-optimal) rational choices occurring due to lack of information. The second story shows fallacious decisions taken by the voters based on *extra* information.

In one experiment (Dillman 1999), a group of subjects (in a US setting) were first asked whether American journalists reporting from a foreign country should enjoy journalistic freedom or obey local rules regarding journalism. Most of the respondents chose the former, stating that American journalists should enjoy journalistic freedom as provided to them in America even if they were in a foreign country. The subjects were next asked whether foreign journalists in America should be allowed to report news stories even if the government feels that they should be restrained from doing so. Most of the respondents felt that it is only fair for foreign journalists in the US to enjoy whatever freedom their home country offers them.

A second set of subjects was asked the same question in the reverse order. They were first asked whether foreign journalists should enjoy unfettered freedom in reporting American matters from America even if the government feels otherwise. Most of them opined that it should not be so, and journalists should respect the law of the land. Now when asked whether American journalists should obey the law of the land on foreign locales, the subjects opined that this was only fair.

The order in which the two questions were asked seemed to create two diametrically opposite reasoning processes!

Lawyers know the above phenomenon well. A question or a series of questions that moulds the reasoning process of a subject are called *leading questions*. Leading questions contain selective information that moulds the listener into thinking in certain directions. The information provided by the questioner may be incomplete and the subject may also be aware of this fact. But coupling an appeal to make a decision with a selective piece of information can distort the reasoning process.

In the Dillman experiment, each question gave only partial information by masking what the next question would be. Had the questioner provided the subjects both questions simultaneously, the response may have been consistently one way or the other.

Politicians sometimes use this tactic for obtaining favour-able opinions. Consider an argument: "Would you vote for the opposition candidate who has corruption cases pending against him in the Supreme Court?" Many times, such an argument works in moulding voter opinion, even though the voters may be aware at the back of their minds that the speaker himself has pending corruption cases against him. If they are asked to form an opinion immediately after the fact is presented, the other facts seem to take a back seat momentarily.

The reason for correct information leading to incorrect conclusions is correlated with the *timing* of information. Human beings attribute a value to every piece of information that they receive. A piece of information seems to be assigned the highest value as soon as it is received and its value is reduced to its proper value over time by comparing it with other facts, observations and conclusions that have been made. If the new piece of information is followed by a pressure on the person to come to an immediate conclusion, then the high value accorded to the new information masks the importance of other facts and conclusions, thus leading the person to come to a wrong conclusion.

Scientists working on artificial intelligence and robotics discovered this in their own way (see Brooks 1999). Conventionally, the widely accepted model of human interaction with the external world was something like Figure 3.1.

The external world is perceived by our sensory organs, which then provide input to our brain. The brain performs the appropriate cognitive tasks of understanding the sensory inputs and formulates a response, which is then given out to the external world in the form of actions.

However, such a model becomes infeasible for all but the simplest of tasks. Even fast computers cannot compute fast enough to give responses in real time.

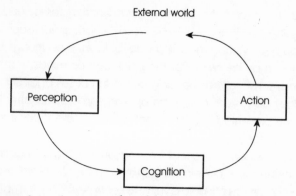

FIGURE 3.1 Conventional model of human interaction with the external world

The conventional model of human cognition is now replaced by a newer version as shown in Figure 3.2.

According to the new model, cognition happens at different levels. At the lowest levels are emotional responses that immediately connect perceptions with appropriate actions. However, as the brain matures, higher layers of cognition develop which *mask* responses from lower layers to give a more measured or "mature" response.

Each layer analyses more information than the layers below it. Emotional responses usually involve very little information other than inputs from the sensory organs. A mature individual for example, would give a measured reaction in response to a situation even though he or she may feel strong emotive reactions. A higher level of cognition would have analysed much more information than what is perceived by the situation and decided on the measured response.

This new model has shown to be enormously more successful in being able to build autonomous rational agents and robots. Not every stimulus requires detailed cognitive

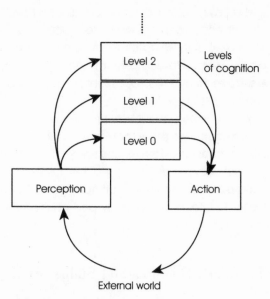

FIGURE 3.2 The new model of human cognition

analysis; and higher forms of cognition are simply added as new layers over existing forms of cognition.

Given this model of human cognition, it is also easier to understand information-related fallacies. If a piece of information is provided along with a pressure to come to an immediate decision, we would have effectively elicited a response from a lower layer without allowing higher layers to analyse the situation more deeply.

Often these distortions are so subtle that the subject is completely unaware of the piece of information that is affecting his/her reasoning process. Several psychological studies have shown that humans exchange much more information during a conversation than what is explicitly seen. Simple things like the changes in expression and tone of a television anchor while talking about electoral candidates have been shown to influence voter decisions (see Gladwell 2000 for more examples). In these cases, there were no explicit pressures on the viewers to come to immediate conclusions. Just the sustained subtle messages sent out by the TV anchor were enough.

While we are talking about how presence of information can cause fallacies, we should not forget that lack of information leads to fallacies just as well. The solution to the problem of judgement distortion due to constant exposure to news is not to completely cut ourselves off from news. This would simply lead to information scarcity and cause fallacious reasoning once again.

3.3 Prisoner's Dilemma and Stable Strategies

Let us now turn to the other pertinent topic that is more commonly seen: how the *absence* of pertinent information affects rational choices.

A widely cited analogy in this regard is the problem called "prisoner's dilemma". Two prisoners are charged for a joint crime, but the prosecution does not have enough evidence to convict the two. The two are placed in separate cells and interrogated separately. They are given a few choices. If both prisoners confess to the joint crime, they face 10 years in prison. If on the other hand, one of the prisoners confesses to the joint crime and the other refuses to, then the one who confesses gets a lean sentence of five years and the one who remained adamant has to face 20 years in prison. Of course, if none of them confess no charges can be proved and they go free.

Each prisoner now faces two choices: to confess or not to confess. If he confesses, the greatest risk he faces is 10 years in prison. This is when the other prisoner also confesses. On the other hand, if the other does not confess, then he gets to face five years. So, the average risk is $(10+5)/2$ which is 7.5 years.

On the other hand, if a prisoner decides not to confess, then in the worst case, he faces 20 years in prison. In the best case of course, he goes away free. The average risk is then $(20+0)/2$ which is 10 years.

Thus rational choice directs each prisoner to choose the former option, since the overall risk is lower. The latter option has a lower risk, *provided* the other prisoner behaves in a certain fashion. But, neither prisoner has any control over how the other behaves. Both prisoners, being rational creatures, confess and face 10 years. Given the fact that each prisoner does not know the decision of the other, such a decision is locally optimal. However, it is clearly sub-optimal globally. The overall optimal situation is when both of them decide not to confess, which is least costly.

Prisoner's dilemma is a prime example of how communication (or the lack of it) among actors of a system can affect individual rational choices. The lack of communication between the actors leads each actor to adopt a "stable" strategy—one which has the least overall risks, regardless of how the other actors behave. However, individual actors pursuing such an optimization locally may not automatically correspond to the global optimal condition for the system.

A variant of the prisoner's dilemma called the "iterated prisoner's dilemma" is known to be applicable to a vast variety of decision-making processes that are made in the face of uncertainty (see Axelrod 1985 for an extensive look into the iterated prisoner's dilemma).

Almost always, human reasoning is situated in an "open world". Reasoning is based on several factors of the external world which we may not be able to predict or influence.

Reasoning in such environments can be modelled by a series of prisoner's dilemma cases. An actor in the system adopts a "strategy" for dealing with open worlds. Each strategy may incur some costs and/or provide payoffs depending on the situation. The best strategy of course is one, which gives the highest *overall* payoff.

For individuals in general life, a strategy is simply the individual's philosophy on how to live. Some people may adopt an aggressive "go and get what you want" philosophy in life, whereas others may adopt a more passive "live and let live" philosophy. The underlying idea behind these philosophies is to minimize the *overall* costs and/or maximize the *overall* benefits over the lifetime of the person. The philosophy towards life need not be restricted to people. Organizations and communities may just as well adopt an overall philosophy for dealing with an uncertain world.

Let us go back to our example from Chapter 2 of mobile service providers vying for a market share. Let us say that there are several companies now, and each company competes with every other company for a share in the mobile services market. Competition involves investment and hence is costly. In addition, if a company loses market share in a competition, the costs it incurs would be even more. The company which wins the competition also incurs the cost of the competition, but the payoffs from winning would be far higher than the costs of competing.

Each company that enters the fray now has to compete with every other company. Because, the opponent's moves are unknown, each company needs to have a *strategy* for competing.

Let us first begin with some simple strategies. The first strategy may be called "bullish" or "aggressive". In this strategy, the company in the fray spares no expense at going into an all out offensive for getting market shares. The company does not hesitate to invest in advertising, discount schemes, buyouts and whatever it takes to expand its marketing share. The company never gives up in this battle, and only stops fighting when it wins or when it is completely rooted out of the market.

Now if all companies in the fray were to be bullish, we see a very fierce battlefield. Each player makes all possible investments into marketing their service and never gives up until they either succeed or are rooted out by the competition.

On an average, if we assume that every company loses half its battles and wins the other half, we can conclude that the total payoff for the bullish strategy is midway between all the profits incurred when the company won and all the losses incurred when the company lost. If the profits of winning market shares are several orders more than the losses incurred by being rooted out, the strategy makes overall sense.

On the other hand, consider an alternative strategy, which we will call "defensive". The defensive strategy is primarily one minimizing losses. When a defensive company is confronted by competition, the company tries its best to get its market share, and gives up after a while, rather than wait for being completely rooted out. Giving up on a battle makes the other party the winner; however, the losses incurred by the losing party is substantially smaller than if it were to be completely rooted out.

Consider now a market solely comprising defensive companies. Each company, on being confronted by another, tries to get its way for a while, and then simply gives up. How long does one wait, before giving up may vary from player to player and from one individual battle to another. Indeed, a player must not be predictable in giving up. If a player is known to give up after (say) one week, the other player simply needs to wait for a week in order to win the battle.

Again, if we assume that on an average, a company wins half of its battles and gives up on the other half, the overall payoff would be the average between its total profits from success and costs incurred in all battles that were given up. Since the cost of giving up is much lesser than the cost of being completely rooted out, the average overall payoff would be much higher than the average overall payoff in a society full of bullish companies.

We can see this as a "proof" of the folk wisdom that peaceful societies are more prosperous than belligerent ones.

But things are not that simple. Consider that a single bullish company enters a society of defensive companies. Easily, we can see that the bullish company wins every battle that it fights with other companies. Its overall payoff would be very much higher than the average payoff in the society, since it only wins battles. The success story of this company would in turn lures other bullish companies to "capture this market" and before long, bullish companies would dominate the society, all fighting one another fiercely.

Hence, while the defensive strategy definitely leads to a prosperous society, it is not a *stable* strategy. Aggressive incumbents who do not share the society's philosophy of peace can easily overrun it.

But how is the stability of a society of aggressors? Is an aggressive society a stable society even though its overall payoffs are lower than the peaceful society? Consider a society of aggressive players where each player fights till the end in any battle. The average payoff for players is the average of all the successes gained and the costs incurred in defeat. Now, consider the case that a single defensive player enters the society. The player gives up on all battles and ends up with the costs of giving up.

Depending on what is the cost of being defeated and the gains of success, the average payoff for the defensive may actually be better than the average payoff of the aggressive others. If the cost of defeat means bankruptcy, or worse (e.g., social and political backlash), it may actually be an attractive option to simply give up on battles that are not worth the effort. When that is the case, the society slowly gets attracted to the defensive strategy. Of course, it cannot completely become a society of "defensives", since even one aggressor in a society of defensives stands to gain. The society settles down to some intermediate ratio of aggressors and defensives. Of course, depending on how quickly members of the society change strategies, it may never settle down and keep oscillating or display bifurcations and become chaotic, as we saw in the previous chapter.

Hence, a society of intensely competitive players need not necessarily be stable. Depending on the payoffs and the costs of defeat, it may attract some defensive strategies or become chaotic. One way to see this phenomenon is as a "proof" of the commonly held belief that not all competition constitutes "healthy" competition. Just removing all controls in a society in order to make it "competitive" does not automatically mean that the society will prosper.

Several such strategies have been explored, and one of the most stable strategies seems to what may be called *retaliating* strategy or "tit-for-tat" strategy. The retaliator follows the following principles: (1) By yourself, be nice to others and don't attack; (2) In a confrontation, do not be aggressive as long as the other party is not aggressive; and (3) Retaliate with an aggressive strategy, if the other party becomes aggressive.

In other words, the retaliator works like a defensive and lives in peace as long as there is no threat of aggression. On encountering a threat of aggression, the retaliator does not give up like a "pure" defensive, but starts behaving like an aggressor. The retaliator strategy is found to have the best overall payoff, no matter how the others in the system behave. It is also a stable strategy in that, other strategies cannot easily overwhelm a society of retaliators.

The notion of stable strategies is very important in formulating policies. Many times, rules are formulated and the people are expected to "abide" by them voluntarily. This is analogous to a society of defensives, where everybody is "expected" to give up their contention after a while. That never happens. Such a strategy is not a stable strategy. If there is a way of obtaining a higher individual payoff by breaking rules, eventually someone will do so.

Such a problem is apparent in the pertinent issue of *piracy* of software, movies and music. Every CD comes with an end-user licence agreement (EULA), which usually forbids the user from making unauthorized copies of whatever the CD contains, be it software, video or music. But this never happens. If people stand to gain from making unauthorized copies, somebody or the other will make it anyway.

The instability of this strategy can be addressed by stricter enforcement of the EULA and preventing copyright violations. However, this is effective only as far as the enforcement is effective.

For certain kinds of software, however, there is a more stable strategy. This involves allowing or even encouraging the users to make copies of the software that is given out. However, the software that is given out would have very limited functionality and won't be of much use in itself. In order to make the software really useful, it would need to access additional services from the company over the Internet. Every such service that is accessed is billed to the user.

Such a stable strategy is possible because software is information as a service. It is not workable for music or videos where the information content is consumed or reused.

3.4 Evolutionary Models of Ideas

The concept of a stable strategy can be generalized to that of an "evolutionarily" stable strategy or ESS. In order to understand ESS it is first important to learn about an evolutionary model of ideas called "memetics".

The term "memetics" was first coined by Richard Dawkins in his famous and controversial book *The Selfish Gene* (see Dawkins 1989). The building block of memetics is the concept of a "meme" which for our purposes is no different from an "idea". A meme is actually a collection of ideas that have a strategy for replicating themselves. For our purposes, let us not introduce new terms, but rather understand a meme as simply an idea. The dynamics of ideas in a human population follows very similar patterns to that of evolution and the Darwinian natural selection.

Genes that are the building blocks of an evolutionary process, function with a fundamental objective of "living" as long as possible. This is achieved by replication of genes during reproduction and thus passing them from generation to generation. The main "challenge" that genes face is the challenge of natural selection. Some combinations of genes seem to fare well in the world, while other combinations seem to be susceptible to disease, short life spans or inabilities to replicate.

As a result, the evolutionary process can be seen as "survival of the fittest". The fittest in this sense is a *combination* of genes, rather than individual genes.

Genes can be seen as formulations of different survival strategies. The encoded strategies in the genes build different kinds of human bodies. If the strategy is stable, the body is healthy and resilient to diseases, while if the strategy is unstable, the body is susceptible and can be overrun by diseases and other challenges.

It is not too difficult to see that ideas and all its associated concepts like innovations, culture, fads and social norms also behave in a similar fashion. While genes are constantly competing and undergoing a selection process at a biological level, ideas are also being subjected to constant competition and selection at a social level. While genes express themselves in a combined form to create organisms with certain traits, ideas express themselves in combined forms like culture and norms with specific characteristics.

While genes face natural selection based on the survivability of the organism that they have built, ideas face natural selection by the kind of payoffs that it has for the holder of ideas. A successful gene replicates by reproduction, while successful ideas replicate simply by copying.

Genes replicate only by physical reproduction, while ideas replicate by communication. Genes require living beings as their carriers for reproduction. Genetic reproduction is subject to all the physical constraints that any material transaction has. With today's technology, it is not possible to combine genes of two people living in far away countries, except if the genes are physically transported. Ideas on the other hand, can have several carriers such as books, radio, television and computers. In fact, the spread of ideas need not require physical activity and all its associated limitations.

Ideas spread in vast numbers and much more quickly than genes.

Some ideas readily combine with other ideas and become stronger in terms of their payoffs. In other cases, ideas compete and clash with one another for attention. Both of the above "strategies" for survival are also seen in genes. Some genes "latch on" or readily combine with other genes, while in some other cases, some genes may "mask" the effect of one or more other conflicting genes in a creature. The masked genes sometimes suddenly express themselves after some generations when the effect of the masking gene has weakened. A similar behaviour is also seen in social settings. Fashions, fads and cultural norms of a long bygone era sometimes come back with renewed vigour for no apparent reason.

That strategy used for survival depends on a number of factors and has different outcomes. If a survival strategy is not good in a given setting, it is eliminated by losing favour among the population.

Some examples are necessary to illustrate the evolutionary properties of ideas. At one time, there was a belief that satellite television and the Internet constitutes "invasion of foreign culture" eroding our own cultural moorings. While they are true to some extent, we see that several of our cultural motifs have readily combined with the new ideas put forth by satellite television and the Internet and have only become stronger. We have temples performing "online *pooja*" services and catering to a globally dispersed audience. Similarly, TV programs in regional language are beamed nationwide and even worldwide using satellite television, thus catering to the linguistic population that are dispersed across the country and the world. These are some examples where existing ideas have combined with new ideas and enhanced their own survivability.

On the other hand, of course, there are several examples of conflicting ideas competing for acceptance. There were a number of agitations against events like the "Miss World" competition and the opening of global restaurant chains like "Kentucky Fried Chicken" in Bangalore, stating that they "corrupt" our culture or established set of ideas. Whether "right" or "wrong" one of these conflicting ideas have dominated and effectively masked the other.

What makes an idea survive and replicate depends largely on its survival strategy and how the strategy fares in the society around it.

Survival strategies in an evolutionary setting are slightly different from the kinds of strategies we saw in the previous section. In an evolutionary system, a "good" strategy may quickly replicate itself through the system. However, this very replication and vast increase in numbers may saturate and bring down the entire system, and the idea along with it.

In genetic systems, there are examples when abundance in food supplies has resulted in a sudden explosion of locust population. The locusts increase in such vast numbers that soon, their population poses too big a pressure on the recourses and there is mass extinction.

On a parallel note, a "bad" strategy may be shunned by the system and may not be replicated. This may in turn work in favour of those holding the "bad" strategy by giving them access to vast resources and little competition.

We have seen the "population equation" in Chapter 2 that can model a class of such evolutionary processes.

A strategy is *evolutionarily stable* if it can continue to remain in existence, regardless of how the evolutionary forces behave. Evolutionary forces are saturation influences in action. Success breeds onto itself and can become "too successful" while a failure may suddenly find himself suddenly being the winner with the most overall benefit.

ESS dynamics are seen very often in the movie industry. A very successful movie on a certain theme results in a spate of similar movies on the same or similar themes from other producers. Often, there are so many such replications that the viewer population gets bored and the theme fails. However, in the midst of this melee, we can often find some directors who consistently produce movies that are successful. Their ESS would be far more complex and intricate than simply pursuing a theme that is labelled as popular by the audience at some point in time.

The idea of an ESS is very profound, and to prove that a strategy is *evolutionarily stable* would be to nail down questions of what is a better strategy *for the long term* in the face of an uncertain external environment. A person adopting an ESS for say, managing his/her finances may never be the richest person among his/her circles. However, when aggregated over a lifetime, the person with the ESS would have had the least number of financial crises.

The idea of an ESS is very appealing as a panacea for uncertainties. Whatever be our challenges, all we need to do is to find an ESS. However, obviously things are not that simple. First, given a system with uncertainties there are no reliable means of enumerating all possible kinds of uncertain situations one can encounter. To some extent, we can figure this out by looking at some of the major exigencies that have occurred in the past. Hence, for a weatherman in a city like Chennai or Mumbai, some of the "expected" exigencies would be heavy rains, storms and high temperatures. While strategies on town planning are developed (or *should be* developed) keeping in mind the above exigencies, a tsunami had not been featured in the above picture—until recently. Several plans that were arguably evolutionarily stable in the face of hot summers and wet monsoons among a host of other factors may have failed in the face of a tsunami.

Second, even when we have decided on a set of exigencies, there are no precise techniques to determine whether an ESS exists for this system and if so what is it or how do we find it. There are no reliable means to measure how a given strategy fares with respect to others in terms of its evolutionary stability.

The best tool we have until now is simulation. Several different strategies can be formulated and simulated for their overall payoffs and costs. Even then, the number of different combinations that one needs to consider for strategies complementing and competing with one another is so high, that it can easily overwhelm powerful computers. (I wonder whether our administration uses *any* kind of dynamics model at all, let alone a non-linear frictionless model, before approving projects like apartment complexes and townships in big cities. Do they even consider the impact that large-scale construction projects have on city infrastructure?)

We usually have to try different combinations based on some heuristics and settle for a strategy that is "good enough" to be considered evolutionarily stable. This brings us to the next major issue regarding information and rationality: bounded rationality.

3.5 Satisficing Behaviour

Ideally, rational choice is a process that is carried out after objectively considering all factors that affect choices and their individual payoffs. We also know that there are several impediments to rational choice like prejudice, dogmas and information-related limitations like ignorance or timing of information.

However, in addition to all of these limitations, human rationality is known to be *bounded,* even in settings that might be termed ideal. As early as 1955, the mathematician, economist and computer scientist *par excellence*, Herbert Simon, had proposed the concept of "bounded rationality". When making rational decisions, humans rarely consider all alternatives to maximum precision, and arrive at the best possible answer. This is so even when they are not swayed by prejudice or emotion, and even when they know they can have all possible information with them.

Human reasoning is often dictated by a notion of "satisficing". Satisficing is the idea of coming to a rational conclusion that is "good enough" for the present purpose.

Consider a case when you are searching for a good bargain on a mobile phone. A typical search would include looking at newspaper advertisements, asking friends, enquiring at a couple of stores selling mobile handsets and searching on the Internet. However, rarely do we ever explore *all possible* options before coming to a conclusion. This is because the very activity of gathering relevant information to make a decision itself poses some cost in the form of effort, time and money. Beyond a certain point, it would not be worth our effort to pursue with information gathering. At this stage, we say that the data we have are "good enough" and arrive at a conclusion.

Similarly, the probability of some events is so rare, that it would not be worth the effort to calculate the benefits or costs of such events. The tsunami issue considered earlier is an example. One can safely bet that not many people who bought houses along the seaside in Chennai would have ever factored the costs of facing a tsunami. First, many of them would not even be aware of what is a tsunami; even if they were, the probability of being hit by a tsunami in Chennai were so rare that it would not have figured into their rational choice.

There are several kinds of satisficing behaviour displayed by humans. For instance, they could be in the form of "giving up" the pursuit for the best solution after a while. In other cases, they could be in the form of assigning local priorities in order to converge quickly to a good enough solution. A commonly seen example of this is the "herd" or "group" behaviour. This behaviour is so common and so potent, that we will be devoting the entire next section on this phenomenon.

3.6 Conformance and Cartels

One of the most common examples of satisficing behaviour is in the way individuals act in a group. The simplest group has at least two people. For group behaviour, rationality of the group should extend beyond the rationality of the individuals making up the group. Members not only contribute to the group's characteristics by their own behaviour, but they also *conform* to the group's characteristics by masking some of their own behaviour. If members of a group were to be studied in isolated settings where they do not interact with other members of the group, their behavioural characteristics would generally be quite different from that of their behaviour in the group.

How are groups formed? One of the motivations for group formation is a satisficing condition in which an individual simply accepts decisions taken by others to compensate for his/her own bounded rationality. How an individual selects other individuals to accept their opinions forms the basis on which different kinds of groups emerge. Thus, we have groups that are formed on the basis of faith, formal written-down rules, geographical proximity, age, shared interests, and so on.

A person enters a group either by choice or by default. Sometimes a person may not even be aware of his/her membership in a group or the way the group moulds his/her rationality. Motivation for people to join groups stems from the sense of safety and assurance that the group offers by compensating for the individual's own bounded capacity for reasoning. Membership to any group, whether it was by choice or by default, comes with its own demands for "conformance". A group evolves its own set of beliefs and norms, and all group members are expected to conform to them. This expectation need not be explicit; indeed, no specific person from the group may enforce these norms. But, the pressure to conform is always there.

An experiment conducted by the social psychologist Solomon Asch called the "conformity experiment" is interesting in this regard.[1] Asch conducted a simple group experiment comprising of eight subjects. The subjects were shown a set of lines similar to the one in Figure 3.3 and were told that they were subjects of an optical illusion experiment. The figure comprised of four lines labelled "A", "B", "C" and "D" and the subjects were asked, which of the lines "B", "C" and "D" was closest in length to "A". In Figure 3.3, the correct answer is obviously line "D".

The actual experiment of Asch had nothing to do with optical illusions. In the experiment, among the eight subjects, only one was the real subject. The other seven were

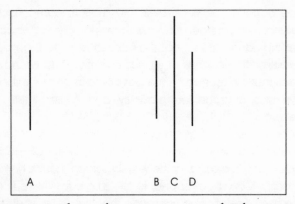

FIGURE 3.3 The conformity experiment of Solomon Asch.
Eight subjects were shown a set of lines similar to the one
above and asked which of the lines B, C, and D is closest in
length to line A. Seven of the eight subjects were "co-
conspirators" who were asked to answer "B", rather than "D",
which is the right answer.

"co-conspirators" planted by Asch, who were instructed to
give a wrong answer (possibly with a suitable explanation
for their answer). The real subject would be asked to respond
last, before which all of the seven other subjects would have
said (say) line "B" is the right answer.

In the majority of cases, it was seen that the real subject
simply went by the group's opinion and agreed that line "B"
was the correct answer! The subjects underwent enormous
amount of inner conflict when they saw that their own observ-
ation and understanding of the question was at loggerheads
with the majority. Many of them simply decided to "conform"
to the group opinion rather than voice their own.

Asch's experiment is very significant for our times. It displays the pressure to conform that people face even when
it is not explicitly stated or enforced. The subjects in Asch's

experiment did not know one another. Neither were they part of any common group with its own norms. The group was formed implicitly at the time of the experiment and just this was enough for the subject to feel a pressure to conform. The reason why people feel a pressure to conform may be many: the prospect of appearing foolish, the prospect of "losing out" in some sense, and so on. Whatever be the underlying reason, conformance is something that few can seem to escape.

Our society comprises different kinds of groups of vastly varying size. Everyone belongs to one group or another. Whether we realise it or not, every day every one of us faces pressures to conform, either explicitly or implicitly.

Groups sometimes exert enormous influence not only on their members but on the larger society as well. An informal kind of group called *cartels* have shown to wield enormous power and influence. Cartels are groups that are formed informally for reasons of convenience, and often operate implicitly. They do not "officially" exist, but they are there, nevertheless, and have enormous influence . Cartels evolve as a result of a number of individual decisions, rather than being explicitly thought of and implemented. No single member is in charge of a cartel, and the cartel itself exists because the members find it more beneficial to belong and conform to it than try to survive independent of it. Cartels have unwritten rules and norms. Sometimes members have no choice; they have to either belong to the cartel or fight it.

Cartels are everywhere and not just in underworld operations, which is where the term is referred to most. Retailers, taxi drivers, oil businesses, restaurants, media, opinion makers, lobby groups, non-governmental organizations and academia are examples where cartels exist.[2] Cartels are primarily groups that are formed for convenience and not really for pursuit of shared ideals. If the latter were to be the case, the cartel would be a formal organization or a society. Remember, cartels are not "officially" supposed to be there.

Cartels work through a network of symbiotic relationships and display great collective power. Many times, cartels are in the news for their powerful *negative* influence. The strong systems of norms inside a cartel often make it impossible for any member of the cartel to think and act in a way that might conflict with the cartel's beliefs. Similarly, it becomes extremely hard for anyone to bring new ideas into the cartel. As a result, the system of thought within the cartel may become increasingly distant from reality over time and the chances of conflict between the cartel and the external world increase.

Cartels are extremely difficult to "reform" as they may not be open to debate or opposing ideas. Individual members of the cartel can be reformed in isolation, but the cartel as a whole is extremely hard to reform. Indeed, many times, individual members display a vastly different set of personal values when they are separated from the cartel. The system of norms within the cartel would have stifled their voices and pressured them into conformance.

A pertinent question for the information age is how cartels would fare in an information-rich society. If it is easier than ever to fulfil our information needs right at our desktops, does it remove the need for cartels? To answer this, we need to look at several facets of this problem. First, what are the motivations for individuals to become members of cartels? One of the primary motivating factors is their bounded capability for reasoning. Rational choice requires collecting information and processing them objectively. Both activities are costly and it is far easier for people to join cartels and reach a satisficing configuration than try to process inform-ation all by themselves.

With technologies like the television and the Internet, pro-curing information is much easier. We are likely to see more examples of informed individual decision making from tomorrow's citizens. For instance, we already see youngsters taking up unconventional career options, having been in-spired by television and searching for their options on the Internet. Similarly, college students today seem to be far more informed about the dangers of activities like drug abuse, something that they were easily vulnerable to earlier.

However, that is only one side of the coin. If individuals are more informed and are capable of taking better deci-sions by themselves, it is also true that cartels are becoming more powerful themselves. Earlier, an individual could be separated from his/her cartel by simply moving him/her to a far away place. Hence, parents who worried about the com-pany that their children are keeping in college usually sent them off to faraway colleges. With present-day technologies like e-mail, instant messaging and mobile phones, the cartel is present wherever the individual goes! The student can be in the new place physically, but still be mentally part of the old peer group. Hence, even with greater individual aware-ness, we would actually see an *increase* in group behaviour. If a person is already part of a cartel (perhaps even without realizing it), the cartel is now able to exert much greater influence than it could do earlier.

Recently, we conducted an empirical study addressing this question (Ramya and Srinivasa 2005). We asked several participants a set of questions. Part of the questionnaire was meant to understand how connected the individual is to today's information and communication technologies; and another part of the questionnaire was meant to understand where the individual is more comfortable with—conforming to a group, pursuing individual pursuits or agnostic to both. The set of questions centred on a major decision-making activity—that of their first career-choice decisions after secondary school. The results were quite as expected by the hypothesis. A majority of the individuals who were not exposed to today's technologies like the Internet, reported that they had made their career choice with no plan, simply choosing the first option that came their way. Their main criterion was financial security. On the other hand, among the subset of the population who were categorized as high exposure to ICT, the percentage of people citing "no plan" had a significant drop. This was compensated by a rise in the number of people who made career choices based on its social standing as well as those who made decisions out of individual interests.

ICT seems to act as an enabler both for individuals and groups. A drop in the number of people having no opinions would compensate this increase in numbers of individual decision makers and of group decision makers. The next generation is likely to be a very opinionated one, either based on individual experiences or group pressure. We are also likely to see many cases of friction emanating from conflict between individual interests and group opinions.

Also, with today's technologies, cartels can seamlessly transcend national boundaries and have global reach. We really may not have much of an idea how many such global cartels exist; how many of them are beneficial to society in general and how many of them might possibly be a danger to civil society.

This might be one of the most potent paradoxes of life in the connected age. Some individuals see ICT as an empowering mechanism for liberating themselves from stifling societal norms. On the other hand, society is also empowered to enforce stricter conformance and on a much larger population. While individuality becomes stronger, conformance and group dynamics also become stronger.

People who are either strongly individualistic or strongly prone to group conformance would find present day technologies empowering. However, for those who want both—individual freedom as well as social standing within a group—it becomes increasingly difficult to face conflicting demands.

In institutional settings, it becomes somewhat easier to ignite the minds of people having a creative bent, and to make them think in new directions by exposing them to new ideas over the Internet. On the other hand, it becomes even more difficult to infuse new ideas into groups. While the number of creative sparks increases, very few would eventually manage to break free from established institutional beliefs.

3.7 Information Commons and the Attention Economy

Just as the prisoner's dilemma relates individual choices to collective optimality, there is another concept in economics called "The tragedy of the commons" (see Hardin 1968).

There is a village largely comprising shepherds. Most of them don't own land. The villagers collectively decide to allot a tract of land called the "commons" for everybody's use in the interests of the entire village. Everybody has a right to graze their sheep in the commons. The commons becomes very popular and everybody sends their sheep to graze in the commons. Eventually however, the grass in the commons starts to deplete. Somebody has to replenish this supply by planting more grass for continued use of the commons. However, nobody has an obligation to do so, and besides, if someone plants grass in the commons, it is likely that others would benefit from it. The effort of planting grass would have no incentive, since someone else reaps the benefit. Worse, when the commons had plenty of grass, there is an incentive for each shepherd to *increase* his flock of sheep. Since grass was freely available, increasing the flock of sheep would be a natural way of increasing payoffs.

Being rational creatures, everyone in the village increase their flock of sheep and abstain from taking the effort to replenish the supply of grass in the commons. Eventually, the commons becomes barren.

The "tragedy of the commons" is extremely commonplace. It is a fundamental argument that is used to advocate the role of governments and public bodies in setting up mechanisms for taxation for maintaining public property, environmental conservation, basic education and healthcare. There is no individual incentive for contributing to maintaining public property; however, without any contributions, everybody stands to suffer.

The tragedy of the commons also brings about a contention that anything of public utility cannot sustain by itself. There needs to be an overarching body that *coerces* every user of the public utility to also contribute to the maintenance of the system.

However, in the Internet age there are a number of cases where this contention does not seem to hold at all. If there is no incentive for someone to contribute to a common pool without a reward, how do we explain the vast amount of data and software that are freely available over the Internet? In fact, the freely available Linux operating system is so popular that it is seen as a threat to mighty establishments like

Microsoft. What motivates people around the world to contribute to the open source and free software repositories, even though their efforts may only benefit someone else?

When the free software phenomenon gained momentum, several people believed that this would be a temporary growth driven mostly by euphoria which would soon die down. This didn't happen and in fact, several business models were developed around the free software movement. Companies sprang up that provided support and maintenance for software applications that users could download freely off the Internet. Other businesses gave away free services in exchange for advertisement revenues.

All these led others to believe that the tragedy of commons is itself fallacious (see for example *The Magic Couldron* by Raymond 2000).

However, there are better ways of explaining why tragedy of the commons does not hold for information commons.

Information exchange is a non-conserved transaction, unlike material exchange. If I give some material artefact to somebody, I won't have the artefact with me. On the other hand, if I give a piece of information to someone, both of us have the information.

Material transactions constitute *movement* of material, while information transactions constitute *replication* of information. Hence, if I plant grass in the commons, others may graze their sheep on the grass leaving nothing for my own sheep. On the other hand, if I contribute a piece of code to the free software commons, I continue to have the software. I have not forfeited anything in contributing to the commons but have helped someone else.

But surely, the argument that a contributor has nothing to lose cannot be enough incentive for investing effort and contributing to the commons. There has to be some kind of *positive* benefit and not just zero loss in order to entice anyone to contribute.

On the Internet, it is quite common to see information as a reusable artefact or service being available for free. Good-quality research papers, blog entries and software are some examples. This is somewhat counterintuitive because it takes enormous effort to write good research papers, blogs or software.

Raymond nicely explains the behaviour of information commons regarding software. Any artefact whether material or information can be thought of providing two kinds of value to the creator of the artefact. These are termed the "sale value" and the "use value". The sale value of an artefact is the amount of wealth you are likely to generate by selling the artefact. The sale price of any artefact is based on the amount of effort exerted to create the artefact and the use it can be put to. Results of manufacturing processes such as cars have a high sale value.

However, because information can be easily replicated, having a high sale value for a piece of software would only result in piracy and unauthorized replication, bringing down the sale value. In fact, unless a company has absolute mono-poly over the market, it cannot afford to have high sale prices for software.

The "use value" of an artefact is the possibility of wealth generation occurring by the *use* of the artefact. The use value of a car for example is the wealth that can be generated by providing after-sales service and maintenance.

When it comes to software, large installations of software have a much higher use value than material artefacts. Main-tenance and enhancement requests for software occur quite frequently. And since software is not prone to wear and tear like materials—coupled with the fact that new software is hard to develop—software artefacts are likely to have a much longer usage span than materials. Even today, we have organizations that use legacy software written almost half a century ago using languages like COBOL running on mainframe computers. Their usage costs are quite high, but it is still low compared to the costs of developing the entire software again from ground up.

Hence, one of the *economic* incentives for contributing software to information commons is to help increase user base for the software. This in turn can increase the likelihood of income generation by providing service and maintenance.

However, this theory of high-usage costs of software still does not explain the motivations behind people putting enormous effort and time in creating very good quality personal home pages, blog entries and research papers for free. Surely, there is no *usage cost* for such kind of information.

In this regard, Michael Goldhaber's theory "attention economy" (Goldhaber 1997) is very interesting. Economics is all about managing *scarcity*. Only when resources are scarce do we have the motivation for assigning prices and creating economies. On the Internet, however, information is not only abundant but overflowing. It is very easy for an average user of the Internet to be overwhelmed by information within a short time.

Hence, using the term "information economy" to explain information exchanges would be fallacious. When there is already so much information on the Internet, what economic incentive would one have to add more to this pool in the form of a personal Web page, blog entry or a research paper?

The key idea here would be to note that the element of scarcity is not *information* but the *attention* of the user consuming the information. Unlike information, which propagates by replication and hence can be in several places at the same time, the attention of a person is limited and can be focused typically on only one thing at a time. The attention span of the average person is small, and an information source needs to resort to several means to keep the reader's or listener's attention for an extended period of time.

Attention is a very primitive human need. Just like food or water, humans display a craving for attention right from birth. And just as not everyone seeks the same amount of money, not everyone seeks the same amount of attention. Nevertheless, just as some amount of money is necessary for survival, so is attention.

Note the colloquial term "paying attention" that is commonly used. There again it denotes a finite resource being provided (as payment) in this activity.

When someone pays attention to my words, I effectively can control some of the thought processes in that person's mind. If for example, I suddenly utter the word "mango" out of nowhere, it is quite likely that you would have seen some fleeting glimpse of mangoes in your mind, had you been paying attention to this paragraph. I was able to make your mind think about mangoes—even if for just a fleeting moment—when you may not even have planned to think about mangoes when reading this chapter.

Obtaining someone's attention is akin to *enslaving* his or her thought processes—even if for a very short duration of time. The term "enraptured audience" is often used to describe audiences who display complete attention to the person on stage. Enraptured is another term for enslavement.

Obtaining attention is a mechanism of influencing rational processes of other people. It may either serve to enhance, limit or skew their rationality. A person gets attention not necessarily due to the rational merit of the arguments that s/he makes. Attention is given for a variety of other reasons as well.

You may have heard the story of the hypochondriac king who believes he has a terrible ailment. Several doctors who tried to tell him that he was absolutely fine were summarily banished from the kingdom. Finally it was the turn of the clever doctor who agrees with the king that he has a terrible ailment and prescribes a medicine with the instruction that he is not supposed to think about mangoes when taking the medicine. This trick ensured that the king *always* thought about mangoes whenever he tried to take the medicine, and finally gave up. The doctor had in effect *enraptured* the king's mind to always think about mangoes whenever he tried to take his medicines! There was no rational merit in associating mangoes with the medicine. But mangoes did get attention, just as well.

On the Internet, when information is flowing in one direction, *attention* is flowing in the other. A property of attention is that, it can be captured and propagated to whoever is paying attention to us. If you are paying attention to this paragraph, I can easily deflect your attention towards mangoes by talking about mangoes.

Hyperlinks on Web pages do just that. If a hyperlink exists from page A to page B, then it not only denotes that the author of page A has paid attention to what is written in page B, but also that the author of page A wants to propagate this attention towards B, to whoever is visiting page A as well.

Consider now that there are two pages B and C, which had content relevant to that of page A. The author of A links only to B and not to C. If a large number of people browsing the Web were to arrive at A, then whoever visits A is much more likely to pay attention to B than C. Propagation of attention thus helps in accumulation of attention at page B. Attention to B is possible by users visiting both the page B directly, as well as those who are visiting page A. On the other hand, attention towards A and C are limited to people who have only visited them directly. Thus B accumulates a larger attention than both A and C.

Celebrities are formed by this propagation of attention. Even when people appear on television or the newspaper, it actually constitutes propagation of attention—from the television or newspaper reporter to us. The reporter had paid attention to some other person and has propagated this attention to others through the media. If this propagation is consistently kept up, celebrities are born.

So in what way does attention accumulate in society? We again see a power law here. Even in a large population, there are a very small number of celebrities that everyone knows and a majority of the population lead fairly anonymous lives. This was true even before the information age, and the power law may only become stronger in the information age.

Notes

1. Have a look at http://www.age-of-the-sage.org/psychology/social/asch_conformity.html for a good description of the conformance experiment.
2. The "Sokal Affair" is a well-known parody in the social sciences. The physicist Alan Sokal apparently got a pseudo-scientific paper published in a reputed academic journal just by using terms that "sounded good and flattered the editor's ideological pre-conceptions." The Wikipedia page http://www.en.wikipedia.org/wiki/Sokal_Affair (last accessed 9 Feb 2006) introduces the Sokal affair and has links to several other parodies in other academic fields. See the article "The Peer Review Cartel" (Malhotra 2004), for another essay on cartel dynamics in academic review processes.

Chapter 4

Information Networks and Cascades

An invasion of armies can be resisted,
but not an idea whose time has come.

—Victor Hugo

It was the year 1995. Information technology was just gaining ground in India. Few people had heard of e-mail and fewer still had heard of the Internet. These were in the exclusive realm of the few IT companies and in a couple of premier institutions like the IITs. Telephone was still under the monopoly of a public sector unit and mobile phones belonged only to the extremely rich. People rarely made inter-city calls using telephone, since it was very expensive; and a vast majority of the country communicated mainly by post.

On a mid-September day—no one knows exactly how this began—a rumour started to spread that idols of Lord

Ganesha are consuming milk offered from a spoon! In less than a few hours, there was frenzy across the entire country. This included not only large metros like Delhi and Mumbai, but even smaller towns and remote villages. Long queues were reported outside temples, comprising of excited, overwhelmed and curious people wanting to offer milk to idols of Lord Ganesha.

People thronging temples created traffic jams in many places. Newspaper offices were flooded with calls with people either wanting to know what is going on, or with people wishing to report their own version of the miracle. Some schools in major cities closed early, fearing chaos in the city. Police went around in patrols appealing for calm. Cable TV, which had just entered India a couple of years ago, suspended their usual programs in some places and started showing temple scenes. Roadside petty shops selling audio cassettes stopped playing their usual film songs and started playing religious songs. Companies that had Ganesha in their name even witnessed brisk trading in the stock markets! Some godmen even claimed credit for this miracle. Rationalists dismissed the issue as mass hysteria, while others saw a "political conspiracy" and/or a "foreign hand". Some newspapers even reported receiving calls from other countries like Argentina, Thailand and Indonesia. All these happened in a single day—no maybe, half a day!

Let me assure you that I am not making this all up. It really happened![1]

4.1 Random Graphs and Connectivity

I am not sure whether Lord Ganesha drinking milk is an idea whose time has come but certainly nobody was able to stop this idea from spreading. It took less than a day for news of the "miracle" to spread across the length and breadth of a large country and even beyond it. This rapid propagation happened at a time when the "information age" was a futuristic dream that was just beginning to materialize, and that too mostly in far away countries. In those times, the Internet was confined only to some software companies, telephones were expensive and people communicated largely by postal mail. Cable and satellite television were there but still confined mainly to cities.

So what does it take for news or ideas to spread through populations? Obviously, a necessary element for propagation of ideas or news is communication among people. The ability of people to communicate with one another is furthermore dependent upon information and communication technologies. In a simple world, people mainly communicate with others who are physically in front of them. With technologies like books, posts, telephone and e-mail, the communication reach of each person increases across space and time.

However, in addition to communication, the *configuration* of the system is just as important in order to determine the spread of ideas and influence. Whenever two people, A and B, communicate, each one can be said to influence the other ever so slightly. Now, if A then communicates with another person C, this communication may indirectly contain some influence of B from the previous conversation. Hence, A forms a link through which B has extended influence to C, even though B and C never communicated directly.

Mathematically, communication networks can be represented by what are called as "graphs". A graph is simply a collection of entities or "nodes" or "vertices" and connections across the entities called "edges". Depending on the context, the connections may mean different things; in our case, an edge between two nodes indicates communication or a possibility of communication between the two entities.

Figure 4.1 shows a simple system comprising of seven entities. For our purposes, let entities depict people in this case. Connections across entities depict acquaintance, to an extent that they tend to communicate often. Hence, A is acquainted with persons B, C and D and tends to communicate with them often. Persons E and G both know F, but not each other. Similarly, C and D know each other, but not B. Hence if D has a piece of news, then A and C get the news directly, and B gets to know the news indirectly through A.

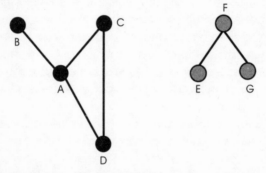

FIGURE 4.1 A simple communication system comprising seven entities (people, for our purpose). Connections show a possibility of communication. The system is partitioned into two; no one from the black group can communicate or influence anyone from the grey group.

We can see that the system is *partitioned* into two subsystems. I have coloured the nodes with different colours for each partition. No one from the black partition can communicate with anyone from the grey partition. Hence, if an idea or news spreads through the black partition, people in the grey partition would be unaware of it, no matter to what extent the idea or news spreads.

Historically, communication between people was primarily by word of mouth. The extent to which happenings in a place could spread, were constrained by geographical boundaries. Occasionally, people transgressed these boundaries and spread ideas beyond their own group. Writing, or putting thoughts on paper, enabled the thoughts to spread much further than the people originating them.

Nevertheless, societies were largely constrained by geographical boundaries. In India, this effective partitioning of the population resulted in a number of subcultures and diversity. Other societies that have developed before the industrial age are also good examples. The Indian subcontinent was rich with several subcultures that developed over several centuries. This was even though the "official" kingdoms many times actually subsumed all of them.

With advances in technology, communication among people became increasingly unconstrained over time. People could communicate across long distances with faster modes of travel and postal services, and telephone and then e-mail. So what kinds of communication channels open up with new technologies?

The simplest way to answer this question is to just assume that communication links develop in a "random" fashion. This assumption brings us to the notion of a "random graph." A random graph is simply a graph structure where edges among nodes are added in a random fashion. For adding an edge, two nodes are chosen arbitrarily and an edge is added between them if there wasn't already one. If there was an edge, then two other nodes are arbitrarily chosen.

As early as 1959, Erdös and Rényi (1959) had showed that such seemingly trivial formulations of societal communication networks display very interesting properties.

For instance, let us consider the question of tracking how far a piece of information can potentially travel in a randomly connected society. This is given by the size of what is called the "largest connected component." Such a component is a subset of nodes and edges of the graph, where every node in the component can be reached from every other node. Hence, the graph of Figure 4.1 contains two connected components: one comprising black nodes and the other grey nodes. An idea generated in any of the black nodes can potentially reach all other black nodes and similar is the case with the grey nodes. In this figure, the set of all black nodes forms the biggest connected component as it has four nodes. The grey component has only three nodes. A connected component might correspond variously to the biggest community or the biggest cultural group in social systems.

Figure 4.2 shows some experiments with random graphs. I have shown two experiments here, the first one with a random graph having 1,000 nodes and the second, 2,000 nodes. In both experiments, nodes were arbitrarily chosen and edges were added across them. After each edge was added, the size of the largest connected component was computed.

Both experiments show a characteristic growth in the size of the largest connected component. Initially when nodes were chosen arbitrarily, chances were high that these nodes were themselves isolated or were connected to only a small number of other nodes. The size of the largest connected component thus remained small.

Largest connected component across random edges

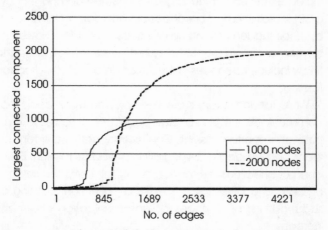

FIGURE 4.2 The size of the largest connected component as edges are added randomly to a graph. Two experiments are shown: the solid line shows a graph having 1,000 nodes and the dash line shows a graph having 2,000 nodes.

Somewhere midway—when approximately 500 edges were added to the first graph and about 1,000 edges to the second graph, we see an "inflection." Physicists call this a "phase transition." As edges are added to the graph, the chances that the chosen nodes being isolated nodes, become increasingly smaller. Similarly, the chances that a chosen node is connected to a large number of other nodes keep growing as we keep adding more edges. Somewhere roughly midway, a randomly added edge would connect two nodes, which already belonged to fairly large communities themselves. Once such an edge is added, the size of the largest connected component suddenly jumps.

In fact, at this inflection point, each extra edge potentially increases the size of the largest connected component by a big factor. The number of people who can be influenced by ideas suddenly shoots up as edges are added. However, beyond a certain point, the system starts saturating and it finally includes all nodes in the system in a smooth, gradual fashion.

While random graphs are a simple model of depicting communication links in a large population, it serves to illustrate an important insight. Connectivity and the extent of ideas and influences never grow in a gradual fashion. Even when connections are formed purely arbitrarily, the spread of ideas and influences witnesses an inflection, causing a sudden burst of changes as communication channels increase.

4.2 Small-world Phenomena

It is not that only with "global technologies" like airplanes, television and the Internet ideas and influences spread across a large part of the world. Throughout history, cultural and religious influences spread much farther than their place of origin.

The fact that humans are interconnected in a deeply complex fashion has fascinated researchers, science fiction writers and artists. In 1929, the Hungarian author and playwright Frigyes Karinthy conceptualized "six-degrees of separation" in his short story "Chains." The notion is that we live in a "small world" and anyone on the planet can be connected to anyone else within five intermediaries using mutual social relationships such as colleagues, family members, friends, and so on.

This concept fascinated many and has been explored in different fields such as psychology, movies, games and more recently, e-mail-based experiments.

In 1967 (Milgram 1967), the American sociologist Stanley Milgram conducted an experiment to verify this hypothesis. A number of randomly selected subjects were given a letter to be sent to a given person whose address was unknown. The subjects were only given their target's name, occupation and general location. They were to pass on the letter to other people they knew on a first-name basis, and who they thought was most likely to reach the target recipient. The subjects were selected from the American Midwest and the target address was in Massachusetts, which was thousands of kilometres away. For the letters that did reach the target it was found that they had an average of five intermediaries!

In 1993, the American filmmaker John Guare produced a film, titled *Six degrees of separation* based on this concept. There was also a famous game called "Six degrees of Kevin Bacon" invented by students of Albright College, Philadelphia in 1994. The game involves finding a link from any movie actor to the Hollywood actor Kevin Bacon. Two actors are considered to be linked (know each other) if they have acted together in at least one movie. An Internet version of the game also exists at the University of Virginia Web site which automatically searches for links based on the Internet movie database (http://www.oracleofbacon.org/). It is interesting to note that almost every actor in the database can be connected to Kevin Bacon in a small number of steps. For example, Amitabh Bachchan is connected to Kevin Bacon by just two steps, and the Kannada actor Vishnuvardhan is connected by only four. This is the case even when there is hardly any overlap in the kinds of movies that Kevin Bacon and Vishnuvardhan act in, or in the kind of audiences that watch their respective movies!

The concept of six degrees, however, is not restricted to celebrities alone. It is claimed to be applicable from *any* person on this earth to *any* other person.

While these experiments are exciting and make for interesting reading, neither of them constitutes a conclusive "proof" of the small-world notion. In Milgram's experiment, for example, only a small number of the letters finally reached the target recipient. A majority of the letters did not reach at all, and this could mean a variety of things: that the letters have reached a dead end and connectivity is not six degrees after all; that the connectivity was indeed six degrees, but the letters could not *find* the best path and were lost in the process; or that some subjects or intermediaries simply lost interest and did not forward the letters. Whatever the case, the large number of lost letters cast considerable doubt on whether everyone can indeed be connected to everyone else by six degrees.

The online Kevin Bacon game does an impressive job of showing the small world of movie actors. If two actors have acted in the same movie, then surely they have some, if faint, acquaintance with one another. However, the game does not say anything about the degrees of separation in the larger world.

A major problem with determining whether we really live in a small world is that the number of connections that can be explored is so large we may not even be aware of where to start looking. Just because we don't find any links between two people it does not mean that there don't exist any.

In the age of Internet and the World Wide Web, there is a large body of information in the form of Web pages and hyperlinks that tell us something about connections in the real world. The set of hyperlinks that connect pages of the World Wide Web can be thought of as some kind of *social* connections, although there are several significant differences with actual social connection. If we ignore the differences for a while and assume that a hyperlink between two Web pages indicates a social connection between the authors of the respective Web pages, a large collection of Web pages may present us an opportunity to verify whether we live in a small world.

One of the early papers on this issue was by Albert et al. (1999), which did in fact suggest a small world structure for the Web with a degree of separation of about 20. Interestingly, a later study with experiments conducted on a much larger scale has shown that the Web does *not* display small world characteristics using hyperlinks (see Broeder et al. 2000). Not only are the Web pages far away from one another there are also parts of the Web that are disconnected and unreachable. However, if we consider hyperlinks bi-directional, then the connectivity of the Web becomes better. That is, if Web page A linked to Web page B, we would consider B linked to A as well even if there were no hyperlink from B to A. There would still be parts of the Web that are unreachable, but connected Web pages are seen to be separated by one another by an *average* degree of six (as opposed to a *maximum* degree of six).

This brings forth several new questions to the small-world problem. One of the first questions is whether random graphs really depict human relationship networks. Human relationships are hardly random. In a random graph, a person is equally likely to know another person on the other side of the world, as he or she is likely to know someone across the street. At least for the ages before telephone and the Internet, this was clearly not a valid assumption. Second, human relationships are also sometimes directional. For instance, I know several things about Amitabh Bachchan, but I'm sure Amitabh Bachchan doesn't know anything about me. What this means is, an idea originating or conveyed by Amitabh Bachchan can probably reach me, but the reverse is not likely. Given the fact that the small-world property breaks down in hyperlinks when the direction is considered, does it affect human relationship networks as well? We shall be addressing these questions in the sections that follow.

But first, why is it important to find out whether we live in a small world? The reason is simple; a network of interconnections depicts how far-reaching the repercussions of any event can potentially be. Connectedness by itself is not an issue. Even without today's technologies, we were in a connected world for several centuries now. Ideas originating in some part of the world have percolated to other far away corners without telephones, Internet or even the postal system. We saw with random graphs that it does not take many interconnections to form a large connected component of the system.

In a small-world network, we have an additional property that, not only can information reach everyone in the network, but they can reach everyone with *minimum distortion*. The greater the degree of separation in a network, the greater is the possibility of distortion. If the world were to be smaller, the propagation is not only faster, but also has more impact. Events happening in one part of the system can have a more direct influence on all other nodes in a small-world network. In the past, major events of Europe like the French revolution had hardly any influence on the lives of most people living in India. However, today a similar major event like the 11 September 2001 attacks in New York has directly affected several people and businesses in India. The same can be said about innovations and other constructive ideas emanating from different parts of the world. A few centuries ago, innovations developed in Europe took several decades to be adopted in India. Now, however, technologies like mobile phones and wireless broadband are diffused in the Indian society almost simultaneously or even ahead of their counterparts in countries where the technologies were first developed.

A small-world network magnifies the impact of any event or innovation by its ability to quickly spread across the system. However, we are still to answer the question whether we really live in a small world. Is ICT really making the world smaller? We do notice that far-away events seem to be having a greater impact on us than they did earlier. But can it be said to hold true everywhere in the world? And even if it did, does a small world network automatically imply that every innovation would have a global impact? Let us turn to these questions in more detail.

4.3 Clustered Graphs and the Degree of Separation

Random graphs are a very simplified model for depicting connectivity. As we saw earlier, in a random graph a person is just as likely to establish contact with someone on the other side of the world, as he or she is likely to establish contact with someone across the street.

This is clearly absurd. When we look at the set of friends a person has, it is far more likely to find mutual friends among this set of people. In fact, historically human societies were largely clustered into communities or villages based on geographic location. In most communities, everyone knew everyone else in the community.

However, even then, and especially more so today, we do have examples of social connections between people living far away. These connections don't have any specific patterns and are best modelled as random connections across clusters. Most communications remain within a cluster, but occasionally ideas traverse these long distance inter-cluster links and influence other clusters. A good example of such networks is the distribution of different language groups across India. Each language developed predominantly inside a small geographical location; however, languages did influence other far-away groups, thanks to wayfarers, migrants and traders.

A *clustered graph* is a much better approximation of human communication networks than simple random graphs. Edges in a clustered graph are not uniformly randomly distributed. Nodes belong to "clusters" where interconnectivity is dense and there are occasional connections across clusters. A cluster represents a context where if a person knows two other persons, then it is very likely that these two people also know each other.

Figure 4.3 schematically shows a clustered graph and contrasts it with a "pure" random graph. In a clustered graph, associations are dense within clusters and rare across clusters. In a "pure" random graph, associations are arbitrary.

In fact, clusters in a clustered graph need not simply represent geographical proximity. A person also need not belong to only one cluster. The concept of a cluster can be generalized to denote any sort of *affiliations*. Hence, a person may belong to different affiliations, like the set of colleagues at work, the set of relatives and a set of friends from his/her interest groups. Each affiliation context, whether it is at work or home, maintains the cluster property that if a person knows

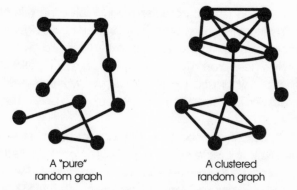

A "pure"   A clustered
random graph   random graph

FIGURE 4.3 A "pure" random graph with arbitrary
connections across nodes, and a clustered graph where clusters
are highly connected within themselves.

two or more people, then it is very likely that these people
know each other.

Information exchanged by a person in one affiliation
group is usually independent of exchanges by the person in
other affiliation groups. Occasionally however, a person
belonging to multiple affiliation groups may act as a carrier
of information and ideas from one group to another.

Such instances denote inter-cluster links from one cluster
to another. For instance, I had a set of fellow amateur radio
enthusiasts with whom I interacted independently of my interactions with colleagues at the workplace. Occasionally
though, someone from the amateur radio group would show
interest in what I do at work and vice versa. Sometimes the
interest is strong enough to form more interconnections
between the set of workplace colleagues and the set of
amateur radio enthusiasts.

With technologies like e-mail and mobile phones, it is believed that the number of inter-cluster connections increases.
In extreme cases, we have examples of neighbours living in

the same apartment complex hardly interacting with one another but interacting on a daily or even hourly basis with people far away. Taking this to its extreme would give us a society where proximity due to geographical locations or affiliations would no longer determine whether people interact with one another. The result would be a pure random graph.

The possibility of cheap communications across the world is also likely to create new *virtual* affiliation contexts. People now associate themselves with online communities like portals and blog groups. Many of them are much more likely to interact with other members of this affiliation context, even when they have not seen one another. So to contend that better communication would result in a pure random graph would not be entirely correct.

Watts and Strogatz (1998) and Kleinberg (2000) studied this question further and showed that clustered and random graphs posses some interesting properties. Clustered graphs can be described at different levels of clustering. At one extreme are graphs, which are simply a set of disconnected clusters. With random inter-cluster links appearing among clusters, the graph becomes connected to various degrees. At the other end are pure random graphs, where clustering is nil and all connections are random connections.

Considering the first extreme, a clustered graph can be a disconnected graph of clusters with no communication across the clusters. Events happening in one cluster do not affect other clusters, even when they strongly affect nodes within the cluster. At a time when society was in the form of villages spread far apart with no efficient means of communication, it was quite possible that some villages would have been making rapid progress in some human endeavour or suffering from some major catastrophe, while other villages would be largely unaware.

However, ever since history has been recorded, civilization was hardly ever in this extreme configuration of disconnected clusters. There did exist connections between clusters and information percolated through these links to other clusters in the system. When connections exist across clusters, there is a potential for events happening in one cluster to affect people in other clusters. The more the number of inter-cluster connections, the more are such repercussions.

However, adding random inter-cluster connections to a clustered graph bring new complexities. Consider two clusters that were densely connected internally. This means that in each cluster the average distance, or the number of inter-mediaries, between any two people was small. Events happening in one part of the cluster, quickly cause an impact everywhere in the cluster, with very little distortion.

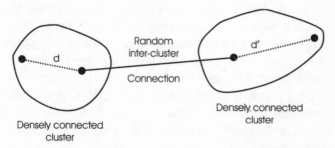

FIGURE 4.4 A random connection between two densely connected clusters increases the overall diameter of the system

Now suppose that a random connection is established between a member of the first cluster and another member of the second as shown in Figure 4.4. This inter-cluster link enables information to flow between the clusters. Events happening in one can now have repercussions in both clusters. For any given person in any cluster, the set of all other persons who can influence him/her suddenly increases when the inter-cluster link is established. If the clusters had 50 and 100 people each, then the number of people potentially influencing any given person would be 49 and 99 respectively. But when a link is added across these clusters, then 149 other people can now potentially influence any person in either of the clusters.

But how "strong" can this influence be? In other words, what will be the degree of separation of the combined graph when this connecting edge is added? To answer that, we have to now introduce a term called the "diameter" of a graph.

Consider any of the clusters. Because each cluster is strongly connected internally, there would be a path from any node to any other node in the cluster. In fact, there could well be several paths between any two nodes. Among these, the "best" path would be the one that involves the smallest number of intermediaries. Consider the set of all such shortest paths between all pairs of nodes in a graph. The longest of these shortest paths is called the "diameter" of the graph. The diameter represents the largest number of hops a piece of information needs to take to reach from any node to any other node in the graph. The diameter is simply another name for the *maximum* degree of separation of the graph.

Coming back to our example, let us suppose that diameter of the two clusters were d and d' respectively (say 6 and 15 degrees of separation). Once the connecting link is established between the two clusters, we can see that the diameter of this combined graph actually increases. If the random link connected ends of respective diameters, the new diameter would be $d + d'$ or 21. However, no matter where the random link connects within each cluster, the diameter of the resultant cluster would be greater than both d and d'. The degree of separation in the connected system is actually higher than the degree of separation in either of the clusters. While the entire system comprising of the two clusters became connected, the connected system has changed from a "small world" to a "big world" because of this.

The greater the degree of separation in any social system, the greater would be the distortion in information flow. Connectivity with a high degree of separation also increases the so-called "*social entropy*". Social entropy is simply the amount of distorted versions of any piece of information circulating in the system.

Activities like establishing business connections not only require connectivity but also low entropy. Consider a set of villages isolated from one another with hardly any communication among them. Now suppose that the villagers are now provided with the privilege of a public telephone by the government. Since telephone is such a rare commodity, it is a community phone residing in the office of the local village head. People in one village can now communicate with people in other villages. But this communication has to go through the single, shared, community phone. Typically, the receiver of a message would not have direct access to a telephone as well. This would require the villager to call up the village head of the other village, who in turn would use one or more intermediaries to relay the message to the final recipient. Such a scenario is not unrealistic at all. Even today, there are such community phones in several remote villages across India. Relaying phone messages existed even in large cities as recently as the 1990s. In those times, the typical waiting period for getting a phone connection was some-thing like eight years.

Suppose people start conducting business over this small inter-cluster communication link. Because each communi-cation has to go through several intermediaries, we may witness increasing accounts of mistrust and miscommuni-cation. When such events repeat, it may lead many to be-lieve that the introduction of telephone in villages has backfired in its plans; or worse, come to conclusions like the telephone is detrimental to villagers' interests, or villagers do not know business ethics, are not mature enough or some such fallacious conclusion. So, a small-world property is necessary if our objective of connecting people is to foster more business relationships.

We can see that if we continue the process of adding random links across clusters, eventually we would have linked enough people across clusters to bring down the overall degree of separation in the network.

Figure 4.5 roughly shows how the maximum degree of separation in a graph varies as random edges are added. Adding a small number of random edges actually increases the overall degree of separation in the system. This rapidly rises to reach a maximum value beyond which, addition of more links will now start to *bring down* the overall degree of separation. So if the degree of separation has gone up be-cause of communication across clusters, we need to keep increasing such communication channels for the degree of separation to eventually come down.

If it is an issue of percolation of news across a population where distortion may not matter, connectivity, rather than the degree of separation, is more important. As long as society is connected, news finds its own ways to percolate

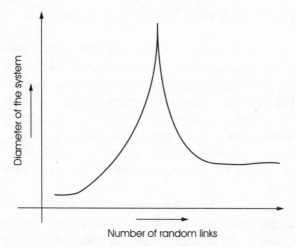

FIGURE 4.5 The diameter of a connected graph as random inter-cluster links are added

through the system. However, when it comes to conducting business, having a small degree of separation becomes important. The greater the degree of separation between any two members of a system, the less likely they are to get into a business deal. Hence, providing remote villages with community telephones and information kiosks primarily helps in increasing their exposure to happenings in the larger world. However, it does not necessarily facilitate increased *business connections* between people of the village and the external world. For this to happen, it is perhaps more appropriate to have a cell phone or a wireless in local loop (WLL) base station set up near the village and offer attractive schemes for the villagers to own mobile telephones. A large number of individual connections are more effective in reducing the overall diameter of the system, rather than large-scale community communication links.

4.4 Kleinberg Connectivity

Jon Kleinberg (2000) addressed random and clustered graphs from a completely different perspective. He observed a not-so-convincing aspect of clustered graphs. In clustered graphs, there are "local" connections among nodes within a cluster and "long distance" connections across clusters. These long distance connections are randomly distributed. A cluster can establish a long distance connection with any other cluster without recourse to where the other cluster is located.

However, human societies always have some notion of *scale* and *distance*. For example, for people who are geographically distributed, calculating distance is straightforward. Geographically distributed societies are categorized into several levels of scale or granularity like localities, towns, districts, states and countries.

Kleinberg was curious to know what new properties the society would have, if interconnections across nodes were to be limited by distance between the respective nodes. To answer this, he created a family of graphs with random links, where the probability of establishing a link was determined by a distance metric called gamma (γ). Gamma represented a decay factor by which the probability of long distance connections decayed as a factor of the distance.

Figure 4.6 plots how the probability of a random link decayed as a function of distance in different experiments, based on the value of this parameter gamma (on a log-log scale, which we had seen in Chapter 1).

When gamma is 0, probability of a random link is not related to distance at all. It reduces to a "pure" random graph. When gamma equals 1, the probability of a random link between nodes decreases proportionally to their

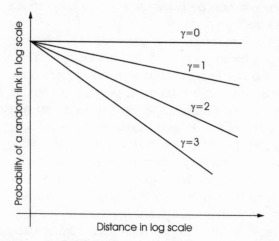

FIGURE 4.6   Probability decay of a random link as a function of distance in Kleinberg experiments

distance. When gamma is 2, the probability decreases proportionally to the *square* of their distance, when gamma is 3, it decreases proportionally by the *cube* of the distance and so on.

At low values of gamma, long distance connections are just as likely as the short-distance connections. However, as gamma increases, long distance connections become progressively less likely.

This brings a curious property to these graphs. When gamma is low, because long distance connections are common, the entire graph has a low degree of separation. Between any two pairs of nodes, there exist paths of short lengths. However, as in the Milgram experiment, for a person traversing the graph in order to find a target person, there is no way to *discover* these short paths based purely on local information. That is, just by asking individuals and following their acquaintances; there is no guarantee that a piece of information can be transmitted from a given source to a given destination.

On the other hand, when gamma is high, there are hardly any long distance connections. Most links from a node end up in the vicinity of the node itself. This makes it easier for a person searching the system to progressively narrow down a search by choosing a neighbour who is closest in location to the destination. However, because there are hardly any long distance links, the overall degree of separation of the graph becomes high. Therefore there would be no short paths between far away nodes in the graph.

Hence, for small gamma, the degree of separation is low. There are short paths, but which cannot be found by local information. For large gamma, paths can be discovered based on local information; but there are no short paths in the graph.

At a critical value for gamma (at $\gamma = 2$), both factors balance one another to result in a graph, which not only has a small degree of separation, but where, short paths can also be discovered based on local information. Such kind of "Kleinberg connectivity" is the ideal graph for the Milgram experiment. Such graphs are not only small worlds, but the small degree of separation can actually be found by individuals and put to use.

An alternate way to view Kleinberg connectivity is to consider the graph at different "scales" or granularity levels. We saw earlier how a geographically distributed society can be organized into localities, towns, districts and states. In a graph having Kleinberg connectivity, the number of neighbours that a node has at different scales is roughly the same. That is, if you have say, three acquaintances living in the same street as yours, you would probably know roughly the same number of acquaintances living in different streets in the same locality, roughly the same number in different localities in the city, again roughly the same number of people in different cities in the same state, in different states in the same country, and so on. If this property holds for most members of the society, then we would have a Kleinberg graph. The society would not only be a small world, but the small world interconnections can actually be found by individuals and put to use. This Kleinberg property holds for me, try it out for yourself and your friends!

Many kinds of human acquaintance networks seem to actually display such connectivity. Kleinberg graphs are well suited for rapid proliferation of information. Given the way the milk-drinking Ganesha rumour spread across the country, maybe Indian society is indeed a Kleinberg graph!

4.5 Information Cascades in Social Networks

Just because a graph has a small degree of separation, or has the Kleinberg connectivity, it does not mean that all information would necessarily cascade across the system. While every day millions of new nuggets of information and ideas are being generated all across India; few if any, have ever cascaded at such a vast scale and at such a speed like the milk-drinking Ganesha phenomenon.

One of the strongest analogies to information cascades is the outbreak of epidemics. Often, the spread of ideas and news is compared to the spread of epidemics in a population. We will see further on, that there are some subtle but important differences between how diseases spread in a population and how ideas spread.

While it is common to see small outbreaks of flu every time it rains, some dreadful outbreaks have known to consume large populations in one go. In fact, at the time of this writing, there is indeed a bird flu epidemic across the world. The bubonic plague of 1347 in Europe lasted for 20 years and wiped out a quarter of the entire population of Europe. A similar epidemic in Mumbai in 1907 killed an estimated 2 million people.

In recent times, we have had sudden global outbreaks of dreadful diseases like SARS, mad-cow disease, dengue and so on. In addition, HIV/AIDS continues to spread in an insidious manner—not exactly resembling the rapid outbreak of epidemics, but not being contained either.

For centuries, people have tried to understand how disease outbreaks result in epidemics. Several mathematical models have been developed to understand the spread of disease in a population. One of the simplest models towards this end is called the SIR model. SIR stands for "Susceptible", "Infected" and "Recovered", respectively.

In the SIR model, a person can be in one of three different states: Susceptible, Infected or Recovered. By default, a population is in a susceptible state in the face of any outbreak. A susceptible person can contract an infection based on his/her *susceptibility threshold* and how many people in his/her neighbourhood are infected. An infected person remains in the infected state for some period during which he or she may infect other susceptible persons. The number of people that an infected person can infect would depend on the susceptibility thresholds of the other person and the nature of the infection itself. Some diseases are far more infectious than others are. An infected person moves into a "recovered" state after the infection has run its course. The recovered state essentially means that the person cannot be infected further (either because the person has developed immunity, or s/he has died due to the infection).

Given a population, the spread of disease is affected by two factors: the average susceptibility of the population towards the disease and the infectious nature of the disease itself. Combining both factors, a mathematical term called the "infection rate" (denoted by R_0, not to be confused with R for recovered state) is introduced. Intuitively R_0 is the average number of other people that an infected person would infect during the course of the infection. This is analogous to the population growth rate r that we saw in Chapter 2.

If the value of R_0 is less than 1 for a given disease and population, it means that the outbreak would taper away by itself. However, if R_0 is greater than 1, then the disease spreads through the population. The greater the value for R_0 the faster the disease spreads and the more the number of people affected. For diseases like HIV/AIDS, the value of R_0 is typically around 2 or 3, indicating that it spreads slowly across a population. On the other hand, diseases like malaria have an R_0 value greater than 100 (see Keeling 2001). Malarial outbreaks can quickly spread across entire populations.

As you may have imagined, a crucial factor in addition to R_0 that affects the spread of diseases is the *connectivity* across people in a social system. The SIR model makes no special assumptions and simply considers that people can make contact with others geographically near to themselves.

With technologies like automobiles, trains and airplanes, this assumption no longer holds. Random, long distance connections between an infected and susceptible pair can cause infections to spread to far away areas much faster. If the random long distance connections resemble a Kleinberg graph, then epidemics can quickly spread across the entire population.

It is easy to believe that information links do not contribute to the spread of epidemics, since they require *physical* contacts between the people involved. But, unfortunately, we have an equivalent of epidemics even in the information world—computer viruses. Many computer viruses are spread by sending e-mails to gullible users and enticing them to open an attachment which promptly infects their computers. Once the computer is infected, the virus sends itself as an e-mail to all users in the e-mail address book of the infected computer. If e-mail connections follow connectivity similar to a Kleinberg graph, it makes it easiest for the virus to spread across the globe rapidly. The gullibility of a user to open a suspicious e-mail attachment would form the susceptibility threshold for that computer.

Social networks witness a different kind of cascade occasionally. This is the cascading behaviour of news or ideas across the population. Urban legends, technological inno-vations, mass hysteria and highly fluid marketplace dynamics can all be seen as different forms of information cascades.

It is tempting to think of information cascades as being analogous to epidemics involving viruses and diseases. There are, however, some important differences. To understand this, we need to go back to Solomon Asch's experiment that we saw in the previous chapter. In the experiment, subjects were shown to *conform* to the opinion of the group, rather than voice their own conflicting opinion. Some subjects, how-ever, stuck to their own opinion regardless of what the group said. In general, the subject tended to conform to group opinion based not on how many people had voiced the opinion but on what was the *ratio* of the people who voiced the majority opinion.

For instance, among the seven collaborators, if six people agreed that line "B" is the correct answer and only one dis-agreed; the subject would be much more likely to choose "B" compared to the case when six collaborators agreed on "B" among a set of not seven, but 14 collaborators. Essentially, the subject tended to agree with the answer that was given by a *large enough* majority ratio of the others.

The same behaviour is known to be true for adopting new ideas. People are much more amenable to adopting a new technology (say, buying a mobile phone) if a large enough ratio of the number of people that they interact with have adopted it. The term "large enough" is a relative term. If a person has five close friends and three of them adopt a new technology, then it is more likely that the person would also adopt the new technology than when the person has ten friends and three have adopted a new technology.

● has adopted the new idea

○ has not adopted the new idea

FIGURE 4.7   Person A is more likely to adopt the new idea than person B even though they have the same number of neighbours adopting the new idea. Person A has a greater *ratio* of his/her neighbours adopting the new idea.

Figure 4.7 schematically shows this. A person is more likely to fall for a new idea if a *greater ratio* of his/her neighbours has adopted the new idea. Of course, whether A actually adopts the new idea or not depends on an internal threshold that varies from person to person about their resistance towards change. But given the same thresholds, a person in a neighbourhood similar to that of A is more susceptible to the idea than a person in a neighbourhood similar to that of B.

In contrast, the spread of disease depends on the susceptibility of the person alone. If a person is likely to contract a disease if three or more of his/her neighbours are infected, then this susceptibility is independent of how many neighbours the person has. A densely connected network is fertile for disease outbreaks and sparsely connected networks contain disease outbreaks within pockets.

In a system that is fragmented, the spread of ideas is limited within fragments. When more communication channels are added, there is a greater scope for ideas to spread. Based on how the graph is connected, the spread of an idea locally may soon reach global proportions and result in a cascade.

However, suppose too many communication channels are added and the graph becomes very dense. Now, whenever a person is exposed to a new idea and is considering whether to adopt it, there is a greater chance of him/her having neighbours who have *not* adopted the new idea. There is hence a greater emphasis to conform to the status quo even when there are communication channels to spread the new idea.

Figure 4.8 illustrates this issue schematically. Suppose that in a population, the threshold for accepting a new idea is 50 per cent. That is, a person accepts a new idea if at least half of his/her neighbours have adopted the new idea.

Now suppose in the system shown in the figure, a new idea originates from node *a*. The idea propagates down to node *h* since half of all the people that *h* knows have

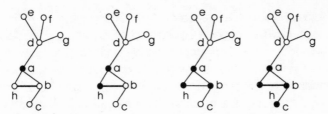

FIGURE 4.8 Suppose that the threshold for adopting a new idea is 50 per cent. Then an idea originating at *a*, can propagate down to *h* and then to *b* and *c*, but cannot penetrate the densely connected set of nodes above.

adopted the new idea. Once *h* adopts this idea, node *b* enters a situation where more than half of all its acquaintances have adopted the new idea, causing *b* to make this transition as well. From *b*, the idea moves to *c*. But the idea never propagates to nodes above *a*. When the node *d* is exposed to the idea, there is a greater (implicit) pressure on *d* to conform to the status quo from the three other neighbours. The number of neighbours who have adopted the new idea is far too small to make this transition.

Social networks that are too densely connected act as inertia to the propagation of new ideas. They implicitly bring pressure on the population to conform or maintain the status quo. This inertia from the neighbourhood is the major factor that distinguishes information cascades from viral or disease cascades. There is an important lesson in here for institution-builders wishing to develop and harness creativity.

In addition, the threshold for adopting a new idea is not the same for everyone in a population. Children and teenagers, for example, have lower thresholds for adopting new ideas than the older population. A cluster of people having the right levels of thresholds and the right connectivity among them can cause a cascade. Such clusters of people who play a critical role are called "percolating clusters". Advertisers have long been capitalising on percolating clusters either consciously or unconsciously and trying to activate them in adopting a new product. For instance, several advertisements targeting teenagers stress on how "more and more" people are adopting this new product being sold. The implicit message here is to create a "virtual" neighbourhood for each person comprising of a number of people who have adopted the new product, thus encouraging him/her to make this transition as well.

A new idea or innovation that is of interest to a population and that hits upon a percolating cluster is poised for a cascade. The idea diffuses through the population with people joining into the set of adopters in rapid succession. If we plot the number of people who have adopted the new idea against time, we obtain an "S" curve, similar to the one in Figure 4.2 that plotted the size of the largest connected component in graphs when edges were added randomly. The adoption of many innovative household gadgets have been known to fit the "S" curve with significant accuracy.[2]

In his famous book *The diffusion of innovations,* Everett Rogers (1995) describes several anecdotes that show the influence of the group on information cascades.

A particularly interesting and poignant anecdote is about how an idea of boiling drinking water before consumption refused to take roots in a remote Peruvian village. Several cases of cholera and other water-borne diseases that were reported from the village were easily preventable just by boiling drinking water. However, the public health inspector sent to persuade villagers to adopt this practice was able to persuade only 11 housewives from a population of 200 families after a two-year campaign! The local belief attributed boiled water to sickness and *looked down* upon the idea of healthy people drinking boiled water. The people who were finally persuaded by the public health inspector actually belonged to marginalized sections of the society. They either were ill themselves, or were recent migrants who were not fully accepted into the society. The main reason for the failure of this campaign rested not in the idea itself, but in the social connectivity. It is not that the people had an inherent aversion to boiling drinking water. It was the social norms that attributed sickness to boiled water that placed an implicit pressure on people to conform to drinking un-boiled water. Instead of uniformly trying to convince people in the village, it was realised that the campaign should have focussed on those who had a high social standing in the society and convinced them first.

Notes

1. See the *Times of India* report on 22 September 1995. This event is also documented online at http://www.theory.tifr.res.in/bombay/leisure/trivia/ganapati-milk.html (Last accessed: 28 February 2006).
2. See http://www.en.wikipedia.org/wiki/Diffusion_of_innovations for a Wikipedia article that contains graphical plots of the adoption curves of several household gadgets. Last accessed: 8 March 2006.

Chapter 5

Information and Money

*Money does not pay for anything, never has, never will.
It is an economic axiom as old as the hills that goods
and services can be [ultimately] paid for
only with goods and services.*

—Albert Jay Nock

The first time I returned to India after a few months in Germany,
I was waiting in the transit lounge of Mumbai airport to catch
a flight to Bangalore. Feeling hungry, I decided to grab a
little snack and ordered for a plate of samosas. I looked at
the price and it said DM 3 (Germany still had Deutsche Marks
then) or US$2, which looked reasonable. But when I saw the
price in rupees, I was in for a shock. A plate of samosas cost
Rs 80!

Of course, Rs 80 converted neatly to DM 3 or US$2 and it is only straightforward that something, which costs DM 3 should be charged Rs 80 according to the prevalent currency conversion rate. What was perturbing is the fact that, had I left the airport and grabbed the same plate of samosas in a restaurant across the road, I would have probably paid only Rs 8. This amounted to about 30 pfennigs—the equivalent of paise in German marks. This is a throwaway price in Germany for a sumptuous snack.

The "poor" people of India who earn only a few hundred US dollars in a year on an average seem to be able to afford the same commodities as people in the "rich" countries. At least, it was true as far as samosas were concerned. A daily wage labourer who earns maybe Rs 50 a day could well be eating a similar plate of sumptuous samosas across the road by paying Rs 8, at the same time when I would have been paying Rs 80 inside the airport.

The global market is a strange system and this strange system is going to bear an increasing influence on our daily activities in the years to come, whether we like it or not. In this chapter, we shall address one miniscule aspect of global markets—namely, money flows in a rational, connected world.

5.1 A Brief History of Money

Money brings about both fascination and abhorrent reactions whenever it is a subject matter of discussion. How is it that little pieces of paper that cannot be eaten, worn, ridden or lived in has become the centre of so many people's lives across the world?

Also, money is, after all, information. What does it mean to transact with money in the connected and frictionless world of tomorrow where system dynamics are sensitive to initial conditions and can easily lead to bifurcations, chaos and global cascades?

To understand these issues, we need to first look into history and understand how the present concepts of money came into being. Whenever we transact with money, there are some implicit assumptions, and it is important to understand these assumptions. Even though this section may look like it is deviating from the main theme of this book, let me request your indulgence in reading it. It is necessary to appreciate pertinent historical decisions that have shaped today's money systems. The main issue here is to see how money systems that are shaped from these mental models fare in the connected world of tomorrow.

Economics is fundamentally about exchange of commodities and services that is of mutual benefit to all parties involved. For want of a better name, let us call a commodity or service that meets the needs or desires of someone as *value*. A business transaction is an exchange, which results in *value addition* for all parties involved. The more the needs or desires that are met for a single person, the more value that is added to that person. Similarly, the more the number of people who report value addition in a system and more the amount of value addition reported, the more prosperous the system is going to be.

In the earliest kind of economic transactions—the barter system, value addition happened instantly. Barter requires the exchange of goods or services that are of immediate need to all parties involved. Even if the parties don't use the commodities or services immediately, they should be aware of their need for this commodity or service. The commodity exchanged in barter should be usable whenever the need actually arises. The commodity should not "perish" by the time it is actually used. Barter exchange provides "instant gratification" in a sense. The barter system is still in use today in several business transactions.

However, the shortcomings of barter are obvious. If I have some commodity X to offer, and am in need of some other commodity Y, then I need to search for someone who not only has Y, but also is in need of X. In addition, the quantities of X and Y required for this transaction should match.

Such shortcomings resulted in a common unit for calibration in the form of money or currency. By using money, one can offer something of value, but defer getting back anything of value. Instead, they opt to receive a "receipt" that can be redeemed for value later.

It is a misconception that money is a representation of the quantitative value of any commodity or service (von Mises 1912). Value assignments to goods and services are subjective and not objective. Suppose A and B wish to indulge in an economic transaction by exchanging commodities x and y respectively. This exchange can happen only if the relative values of x and y are inverted between A and B. A should place a higher value for y as against x, while B should place a higher value for x as against y for an exchange to happen. If a person sells tomatoes for Rs 10 per kg, then Rs 10 is not the value of a kg of tomatoes; rather, one kg is the amount of tomatoes the person is willing to exchange for a quantitative value of Rs 10. For the seller, a kg of tomatoes is worth *less than* Rs 10, while for the person who buys it; a kg of tomatoes is worth *at least* Rs 10 (at that place and at that point in time).

When someone pays currency in exchange for goods or services, the currency can be seen as a *receipt* or *acknowledgment* for the value addition received by the person. In an economic setting, this receipt is widely accepted by a large number of other people, and can be redeemed by the holder for obtaining value from someone else.

Currency itself can take various forms. Between 9000 and 6000 BC, people in different parts of the world used livestock as a common unit of interchange. Cattle is perhaps the oldest currency used by humans; and their use continued till the mid 20th century in some places of interior Africa (Davies 2002). The domestication of cattle preceded the agrarian revolution; following which, even crops were used as currency. Another commonly used currency in several parts of the ancient world, especially ancient China, were cowry shells. Ancient China was also known to use metallic tools like spades and knives as currency.

Any material that is used as currency acts as a carrier of information about the value the holder is entitled to receive. However, there are two major problems with any material that is used as currency. First is the issue of authentication. If written statements are issued as a receipt, then it is possible to easily generate bogus statements to obtain a greater buying power.

The second issue is the durability of the material carrier of information. Crop and cattle perish and become useless after a while. Written statements may be destroyed or mutilated. When currency perishes, the redeemable value associated with it also perishes. As early as 2000 BC, some parts of the world were already addressing these issues by using currency made from light, durable metals and authenticated by the state by a royal seal. The actual metal used for currency varied from place to place and over time. They included silver ingots, gold and other metallic amalgamations.

In most cases, the authenticating agency was also the only agency allowed to mint currency. This continues to be the case even today. Usually the state acts as the sole authenticating agency (by institutions like the Central Bank or the Reserve Bank) for currency.

Technically, an economy need not have just one central authenticating agency; there can be any number of trusted authenticating agencies. Indeed, this was the case in the United States until the early twentieth century. For several historical reasons involving global trade and the gold standard, the notion of central banks have taken root and has stayed that way.[1] However, as long as it is possible to somehow verify that the holder of currency wishing to redeem it for value has actually earned that receipt by adding value elsewhere, economic transactions can happen.

Similarly, the authenticating agency need not actually mint currency. Technically, it can function solely by authenticating receipts issued by people for each transaction. Think of a hypothetical system where person A receives value worth v from person B, with a representative from the authentication agency acting as witness. Person A then issues a receipt to person B for a value v, which is then authenticated by the representative. If all transactions in the system were to happen this way, then there is no "currency" in such a system. The currency is generated at every transaction and is authenticated by someone who can vouch that value addition did take place. This is not very unrealistic; such systems can indeed exist for Internet transactions, and even for some paper transactions using some ICT-based authenticating technologies.

But it is easy to see that such a system is infeasible without fast and reliable information and communication technologies. The easier option is for the authenticating agency itself to issue currency and forbid anybody else to issue the same kind of currency.

When an authenticating agency issues currency itself, a pertinent question that arises is: when can new currency be minted? A currency unit represents an authenticated receipt of a certain denomination. A currency note of Rs 10 can be given away by someone only when a commodity or service of (subjective) value at least Rs 10 is received.

When currencies were made of gold and other precious metals, this correspondence was easy to establish. The *commodity value* of the currency was meant to be the same as its *market value*. A gold coin of denomination x would hence contain gold that is worth x units in the same currency.

However, such a system is vulnerable to what is called as "debasement". Gold coins were frequently chipped off by people to obtain small nuggets of gold for themselves. This reduced the commodity value of the coin, while retaining its market value based on the denomination embossed in it. Sometimes, debasement was done by the state itself to generate more money from less metal. One of the first historical accounts of debasement was by Emperor Nero of Rome who reduced the weights of the silver denarius from 4 grams to 3.8 grams. Debasement made perfect rational sense, as the market value of the currency remained intact, while its commodity price reduced. This had prompted Sir Thomas Gresham, an English financier, to retort, "Bad money drives good money out of circulation." This quote later came to be known as "Gresham's law" that is quoted in several contexts when referring to commodity and market values of currency.

The notion of commodity value of money is pertinent only when material carriers are used for transporting information that money carries. However, money itself is abstract—it is a piece of information representing value, which itself could

take on several forms. What is crucial is that every bit of denomination that money carries should correspond to some
value *that has already been added in the system*. Money
can be generated only in *response* to value addition and
never without it. Unfettered minting of money simply results
in inflation and brings down trade, since a perception
develops that no matter what amount of money is earned,
it may become worthless in the future.

On the other hand, value addition is such an abstract
entity itself. It can take on different forms, and the question
of when value has been added remains elusive.

The "gold standard" that was prevalent for centuries across
several countries addressed this question by establishing a
correspondence between currency and gold. The story of
the gold standard itself is long and intricate. Several theories
exist as to why gold was used as a standard measure of
value. No single event was solely responsible for the gold
standard; but by the end of the nineteenth century, many
countries across the world regulated their money supply by
establishing a correspondence to gold reserves. Much of
the reasons leading to the gold standard are historical—
based on the widespread use of gold, and related to the
metallic properties of gold itself.

The international gold standard not only regulated money
supply and inflation but also paved the way for systematizing
trade across currencies. In a sense, gold was the common
international currency and all currencies that had a correspondence to this standard were inter-convertible. The gold
standard resulted in dramatically increased trade among
the then industrializing nations and other "periphery" nations
from where agricultural products and other natural resources
were sourced.

However, the gold standard is largely dismantled today. The reasons that led to the rejection of the gold standard are many. But in retrospect, we can see that the gold standard is not sustainable. Establishing correspondence between currency and *only* gold makes all other kinds of value addition less lucrative.

Some of the dramatic events of this time include the Gold Rush that witnessed massive migration of people into California in a mass hysteria over finding gold there in the middle of nineteenth century. At the peak of the Gold Rush, people even paid $100 for a drink of water![2] This is an outrageous price even by today's standards!

In the 1845–49 Irish potato famine, exporting food to Britain from Ireland was found more profitable than meeting the acute shortage of food supply locally[3,4] (see Judge 1981). Food supply had no place in determining wealth—wealth had to correspond to gold somewhere.

Many economists, most notably the Nobel laureate Amartya Sen, have argued that most famines occur not due to paucity of food but due to a skewed underlying exchange mechanism. Sen argues that countries should be measured based on an abstract entity called "capability" of their citizens (Sen 1982a, 1982b). Capability can be seen as a measure of how easy is it for the citizens to meet their demands and exercise their rights in the system. In other words, capability is a measure of how well the configuration of a system facilitates value addition, or how easy is it to meet demands with supply. For instance, every citizen of India has a *right* to vote, but not necessarily the *capability* to vote. The capability results from a number of factors— from the very general such as education to specifics like easy access to polling booths and security at the polling booth. From a monetary perspective, the amount of money that a country has should have some correspondence to the "capability" present in the system. The wealth of nations is in their "capabilities" and not in the amount of gold they possess.

No longer strictly following the gold standard, most currencies today are what are called as "fiat money". Fiat money refers to all instruments of exchange that are not backed by any fixed assets, but which are accepted by law as valid instruments of exchange. Historically, fiat currency came into being as a response to shortage of hard currency issued by the government. A shortage of currency to back value considerations in economic transactions led to the emergence of several kinds of "promise to pay" receipts like IOU (I owe you) statements, stocks and scrip. When governments started to accept these instruments for redemption, they were called as "fiat money". Even paper money or bank notes came into being as fiat money.

The main characteristic of fiat money is that it is essentially "unbacked" currency. They are usually created based on promises of redemption offered by large institutions and government establishments. Theoretically, the promises are unenforceable and unregulated creation of fiat money brings down the system. The main backing that fiat money of any country has today is the stability of the government and other institutions in the country. By holding a stable currency, one has a much higher probability of having it redeemed for value than holding an unstable currency.

This brings us to the crucial point of this chapter—namely, what happens or what can happen, when information and communication technologies tightly interconnect several fiat currencies across the world.

5.2 Money as Commodity and the Money Marketplace

The idea of money, of whatever variety, historically has had another implicit assumption. It is that exchanges using a currency largely take place within a bounded geographical cluster. If we draw a graph structure connecting buyers and sellers, the global marketplace historically resembled a clustered graph that we encountered in the previous chapter. Each cluster represents a monetary system—typically a nation-state.

Largely, money would be traded locally within a cluster. There would be relatively infrequent long distance connections where trade happens across different currency systems. The first diagram in Figure 5.1 schematically depicts this.

In the agrarian age, such long distance connections were extremely rare, although they were definitely present in several parts of the world. Because there was no common unit of exchange across currency systems in these ages, there was no single mechanism for trading across currency systems. When sea-faring traders arrived for trade from far away shores, the commodities they brought with them held higher value than their currency. Their currency was valued primarily on the commodity value of that currency. In addition, the commodity value that was assigned depended on the point of trade. Within a single currency system, a foreign currency would have received vastly different commodity values from different traders.

With the international gold standard, much of this inter-currency exchange became systematized. By establishing correspondence between currency and gold, it was possible to precisely calculate and provide an assurance for the worth of one currency inside another system. If one could by a

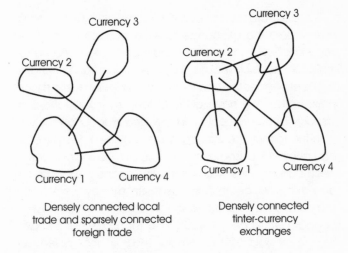

FIGURE 5.1 Graph models of global trade. Historically, global trade resembled the clustered graph. But global trade of information artefacts and services today increasingly resembles a "pure" random graph.

unit of gold using x units of currency C or y units of currency D, then one unit of currency C was worth y/x units of currency D. The establishment of the gold standard vastly increased international trade (or trade across currencies). This was of course, also augmented with technological advances like automobiles, ships and airplanes.

This system was not without its flaws, and indeed the hard currency of the gold standard has given way to fiat money, in order to handle deficiencies in money supply.

The idea of an exchange rate between currencies can be seen as assigning commodity value for one currency in terms of another. This is easy to assign when currency is backed by hard assets like gold. But what does it mean to assign a commodity value for fiat money?

There are two ways to address this question. One is to ask, how *should* the exchange rate be calculated and the second is how *is* the exchange rate calculated when left to individual decision makers. The "how should" question takes a global perspective and the "how is" question takes a local perspective. We have already seen many instances of disparity between local optimality and global optimality.

In the former, the exchange rate between one currency and another is based on the relative *purchasing power* that each currency has in its system. For instance, suppose the only thing we could purchase with money were to be *samosas*, then one dollar should translate to Rs 4. This is because, while people paid Rs 8 for a plate of *samosas* here, they paid $2 for a similar snack in that system. Of course, *samosas* aren't the only thing that makes up an economy, so such a conversion taking just one commodity is inadequate.

The *purchasing power parity (PPP)* between two currencies is a state where the exchange rate between the currencies remains in equilibrium. The exchange rate at PPP or the "ideal exchange rate" is calculated by using a representative "basket of goods" whose prices are normalized based on the relative importance of each good in the respective economy. Of course, the biggest challenge lies in creating this representative basket of goods and finding representative prices for the commodities in each of the two economies.

PPP exchange rates are aggregate measures, the calculation of which requires enormous effort and time. The PPP exchange rate refers to global optimality in inter-currency exchanges.

In contrast, exchange rates often change on a daily basis, based on a number of individual decisions made by people buying and selling currency. The exchange rate is determined partly by the *perception* of each trader of the relative value of one currency over the other. In fiat currencies, the value of a currency is a measure of the probability with which one can exchange currency denominations for goods or services. If one of the two economies is stronger—has more businesses, has a stronger military power, is known to be resilient in the face of crises, and so on—this currency acquires a higher value with respect to the other.

The number of individual decisions or "market forces" that determine exchange rates is ideally supposed to eventually converge to the PPP exchange rate. In a free market, anybody is free to trade with anybody else and biases of any kind are supposed to cancel each other out.

However, we have seen that no matter how well connected a system is, individual optimality need not necessarily translate to global optimality. Individual decisions are prone to several shortcomings like the prisoner's dilemma, bounded rationality and group behaviour. In addition, as connectivity increases, non-linear dynamics also increase, leading to reinforcing causality loops that we have seen in Chapter 2. For example, perception of impending unrest within a country may cause intense trading with people frantically trying to sell currencies of this country. This frantic activity may fuel the perception even further, leading to activity that is even more frantic.

As a result, the *market* exchange rates between currencies are usually quite different from the PPP exchange rates. As of 2004, the PPP exchange rate between the Indian rupee and the US dollar was about Rs 10 to a dollar, while the market exchange rates were about Rs 48 to a dollar. In fact, if the gross domestic product (GDP) of India is adjusted for PPP, India emerges as the fourth largest economy of the world as of 2004; but when the GDP is calculated based on the market exchange rates against the US dollar, India figures as the tenth largest (World Bank 2005).

In a completely unregulated environment, self-fulfilling reinforcing loops during currency trading can be so powerful as to cause a weak economy to collapse. An example is the fall of the Russian rouble when USSR was dismantled. A currency whose exchange rates were artificially held up by the government was suddenly subject to an unregulated marketplace. This resulted in a rapid fall of the rouble against the dollar (and most other currencies). Looming uncertainty in the USSR made investors sell roubles to buy dollars, which in turn fuelled more uncertainty. By June 1992, one dollar cost 200 roubles, and by November the same year, it had become 500 roubles to a dollar.[5]

In order to prevent collapse of their weak currency, some countries *peg* their currency to a stronger currency. This means that the exchange rate between these two currencies remains constant and the weaker currency can ride on the stability of the stronger currency. Several small South Asian countries have pegged their currencies to the US dollar. The Nepalese rupee is pegged to the Indian rupee and the Scottish pound is pegged to the British pound. There are also cases where a weaker currency is abandoned altogether and the economy starts accepting the stronger currency. For example, Ecuador and Panama have adopted US dollars as their currency.

5.3 Purchasing Power Dynamics in a Wired World

As the world becomes more connected, money exchange is increasingly decoupled with material interchange. It is no longer necessary for actual paper money to flow between countries for trade to happen. Electronic payments have made it possible to transact instantaneously across continents. When the commodities of exchange are also information artefacts like software or IT-enabled services, the entire business transaction can be instantaneous and global.

In fact, with technologies like the Internet, it is not only possible to instantaneously transact globally, this transaction can be performed by *end users* themselves. The number of intermediaries in an international transaction have reduced drastically, giving rise to concepts like "the corner-house MNC". Multinational companies no longer mean large corporations with turnover running into the billions. In service sectors and software, several small "corner-house" companies are found to be having operational units in several countries. This phenomenon is already seen in IT hubs of India like Bangalore, Hyderabad and Pune, where several small companies running from houses and garages, routinely or solely conduct business with overseas clients.

In graph-theoretic terms from the previous chapter, a clustered graph is now turning into a "pure" random graph, where random long distance connections may connect nodes from different currency systems. This is schematically shown in Figure 5.1. In addition, the overall *diameter* of the graph is also rapidly decreasing.

Now suppose that the markets are free and only regulated enough to prevent collapse of one currency over another. Arguably, a free market without centralized controls is closest to realizing the ideal of scaling economic opportunities over large populations. However, free trade within a single currency system is different from free trade across currency systems, especially when currency conversion rates themselves are dynamic.

A pertinent question now would be to ask, how increased inter-currency connectivity would affect individual purchasing powers. Would a free market spanning across economies result in greater purchasing power for both economies? Or would one of the economies suffer because of jobs and wealth moving to the other?

In order to study this, let us resort to simulation. Consider a simple version of the problem comprising of just two economic systems S and W. One of the currencies—say S—is stronger than the other. This means that the market exchange rate between S and W is more than the PPP exchange rate.

Whenever the market exchange rate differs from the PPP exchange rate, trading across currencies are subject to what is termed as "arbitrage opportunities". An arbitrage opportunity is the opportunity for profit that can be obtained by exploiting price differentials. A person in system S finds it lucrative to source goods and services from W and sell in S. Similarly, a person in system W finds it more lucrative to sell his/her goods or services to someone in system S, rather than selling it to someone locally.

Hence, there is a rush in S to "outsource" procurement of goods and services to W, and there is a rush in W to cater to the market in S, rather than cater to the local market. However, after a while, some of the early movers in W would have obtained so much wealth locally, they may constitute an attractive market themselves in W. Similarly, when a number of players in S have started sourcing from W, their relative cost savings would become negligible.

So where does it all settle down, and how do we measure the resultant purchasing power in both systems? To answer this question, we need to perform a simple simulation over random graphs. We have a graph with a set of nodes, half of which are labelled s and the other half labelled w. There is an exchange rate r which is the ratio s/w or the amount of w currency units that makes up one unit of s.

In this system, each node (representing a person or an institution) connects to one or more other nodes with some probability. The probability is dependent upon the amount of money that the other node already has. If node A establishes a connection with node B, it means that node A is willing to meet the demands of node B to obtain money. Remember that money is a receipt for value received. If node A connects to node B, it means that node A finds possession of node B's receipt as lucrative in terms of its redeemability. Once a connection is established, money flows through the link from B to A. Again, to simplify things, we assume that B distributes all money it has to all those who connect to it. The node B itself receives money based on whoever it connects to.

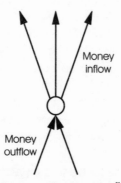

FIGURE 5.2 Simulation set-up. Money inflow for a node is based on who it connects to, and money outflow is based on who connects to it.

Figure 5.2 illustrates the idea. Arrows pointing outwards actually indicate money inflow, while arrows pointing into the node depict money outflow channels. Initially, the system starts with an equal denomination of money for all nodes. However, every denomination of money in the s nodes will be worth r times their denomination for the w nodes.

As and when links are added, money keeps flowing in the system with each node spending all that it has on nodes that point to it and receiving something from all nodes that it points to. This system is left to run for a sufficiently long duration of time and then measurements are taken.

At the end of the run, we need to measure how much each node is worth. How do we calculate the worth of a node? One simple way is to measure the money present in the node. However, this is not a reliable measure since the node may have just made its payments and may not have received all payments. Similarly, the node may have received payments, but not have spent anything yet. A more reliable measure is to look at the *history* of money flow through the node. Since we are not modelling savings or hoarding of money, the history of money flow shows the purchasing power that the node has actually realized over time.

Another way to understand buying power is to see the number of incoming links to a node. An incoming link to a node says that someone else is willing to meet the demands of that node based on the wealth that it has. The more the people that link to a node, the more is the buying power of that node.

However, suppose I have to construct a house and have the following options: supervise a team of 100 labourers who charge less; or supervise one contractor who takes care of the entire construction but who charges more. If I can afford it, it would make sense to choose the latter. Putting it the other way round, if a contractor who himself is worth a lot of money is willing to work for someone, then that someone is worth even more. Hence, the purchasing power of a node is dependent on the number of incoming links and *their* purchasing power.

Purchasing power is hence calculated recursively until the values settle down. In mathematics, it is called the calculation of the principal eigen vector of the incidence matrix between nodes. Web search engines like Google, compute the "PageRank" or the "prestige" of a Web page in a similar recursive fashion (Brin and Page 1998). Surprisingly, taking the history of money flow through each node is shown to approach the PageRank or the principal eigen vector values after a sufficiently large number of iterations (Abiteboul et al. 2003). In fact, in the well-known algorithm called Online Page Importance Computation (OPIC), the economic metaphor that is used here is used for Web pages to compute their PageRank. The PageRank of a Web page in OPIC is simply its "purchasing power".

Figure 5.3 plots distribution of the purchasing power in both the systems. The solid line in the figure represents the stronger currency and the dash line represents the weaker currency. The different plots represent purchasing power distribution at different exchange rates. The exchange rate is measured as the ratio between the market exchange rate and the PPP exchange rate.

At the top-left is the plot that shows purchasing power distribution when market exchange rate is equal to the PPP exchange rate. We can see that, while purchasing power is not uniformly distributed across the system, the purchasing powers of both systems are roughly the same. As the market rate for the stronger currency increases against the weaker currency, arbitrage opportunities set in. For a node in the weaker system, it makes more sense to connect to a node in the stronger system, than connect locally.

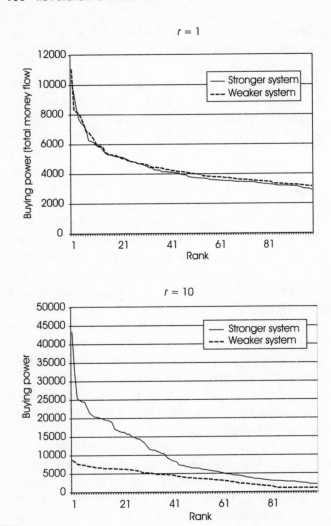

_r_ = 1

_r_ = 10

(*Figure 5.3 Contd*)

(*Figure 5.3 Contd*)

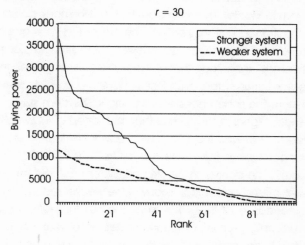

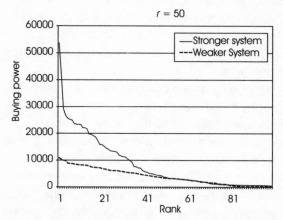

FIGURE 5.3 Distribution of purchasing power across the two systems. The solid line represents the stronger currency and the dash line represents the weaker currency. The graphs represent different exchange rates as a ratio of the market exchange rate to the PPP exchange rate. Row-wise from top: exchange rate = 1, 10, 30, 50.

Arbitrage opportunities make the chances of a node being connected by other nodes higher, if the node belongs to the stronger currency system. This is reflected in the graphs where the overall purchasing power of the stronger system becomes higher than that of the weaker system. When the weaker currency falls even further, we see a curious phenomenon. The richest people of the stronger system still have a much higher buying power than the richest of the weaker system. However, the purchasing power distribution in the stronger system falls quite rapidly from its richest to the poorest. The poorest in the stronger system actually have a *lesser* buying power than many in the weaker system!

The reason for this is that when the currency differentials are very high, some of the early movers in the weaker system obtain large amounts of wealth very quickly by connecting to the stronger system. Within a few iterations, their wealth would have increased so much that they start competing with many in the stronger system for attracting others to meet their demands.

In addition to this, we can also see one more property in the graphs. As the market exchange rate increases, the purchasing power distribution in the weaker system is much more flatter than in the stronger system. For people in the weaker system, the stronger system represents a "gold mine" which can be tapped to provide high wealth for the same or lesser efforts that they need to exert when they connect locally. In a connected world with low transaction costs, everybody rushes for this opportunity. This results in a flat distribution of wealth in the weaker system. But the flat distribution of wealth does not give the weaker system higher *purchasing power* against the stronger system. The stronger system would still enjoy more influence, but it would probably face more internal unrest resulting from widening disparity between its richest and poorest.

Is it any surprise then that the US witnessed a huge backlash against outsourcing of service jobs to India? This is not the first time the US has outsourced jobs overseas. A few decades ago, many manufacturing and production units outsourced to China. However, there wasn't such a big backlash. The current backlash is caused not so much by outsourcing itself but by high connectivity. When manufacturing and production jobs were outsourced to China, the costs of international outsourcing was so high that only large corporations could afford to do so. However, with increased connectivity, global operations and arbitrage opportunities are no longer confined to large corporations. Small corner-house firms can effectively leverage the global search space and arbitrage opportunities so much so that it begins to show on the overall purchasing power distribution. The kind of outsourcing that is happening today is not relegated to high-end engineering projects. There are many companies in India that for example, provide services of homework support for high school kids in the US.

There is a saying that a thousand small cuts on the body are much harder to handle than one large cut. Even though, I wouldn't call business transactions as "cutting" the other economy, it would amount to the same because of the way inter-currency trade is configured. Much of the business connections in inter-currency trade today are about arbitrage benefits rather than being based on core economic principles of value addition and redemption.

5.4 Greed is Bad for the Strong, Worse for the Weak

The model that we saw in the previous section allowed new connections to be formed as and when money flowed through the system. However, it did not allow connections to be broken.

Often business connections are broken for just the same reason why they were made in the first place—to minimize cost and maximize profit. Since in this model, we are concerned with purchasing power and nodes spend *all* their money in order to reveal their purchasing power, we do not have a concept of minimizing cost. However, we can model broken business links based on maximizing inflow.

We started the system with an equal denomination of wealth among members of the system. For a given system, all members shared the same initial probability of being connected. However, after a few initial connections are made and money flows through the system, the wealth distribution of nodes changes. We can now model nodes to be "greedy"—in the sense that if they find that one or more of their business links are contributing too little to their money inflow, they simply break these links and look for better links. The value "too little" is of course parametric and measured against a threshold. Different values of the threshold mean different levels of greed. To make things simple, we assume one convenient value of threshold for the entire population.

Figure 5.4 plots the purchasing power distribution when this "greed factor" is introduced. In this simulation, nodes were allowed to break links with other nodes and look for better opportunities, whenever the other nodes' contribution amounted to less than 1 per cent of their money inflow.

$r = 1$

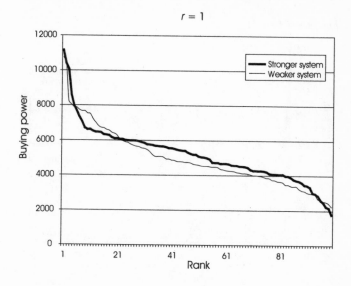

$r = 10$

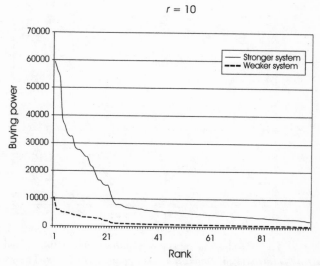

(Figure 5.4 Contd)

(Figure 5.4 Contd)

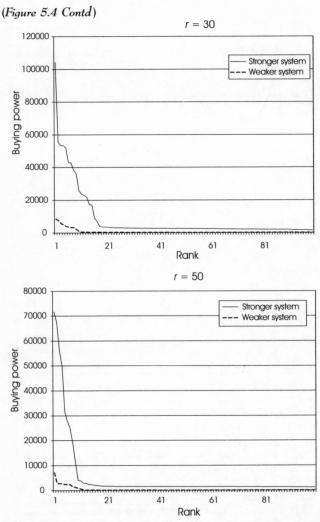

FIGURE 5.4 Purchasing power distribution when the "greed factor" is introduced. Nodes may act opportunistically and break existing business links to look for ones that are more lucrative. Row wise from top: exchange rate = 1, 10, 30 and 50.

Even with such high leniency, we can see that the set of graphs here are quite different from their counterparts from Figure 5.3. Giving up on business ties that pay less than 1 per cent of a large income is very much common; in fact, thresholds are often much higher.

When the exchange rate is equal to the PPP, the greed factor has no effect. Everyone in both systems is just as affected or unaffected by others' greed. The overall distribution of purchasing power for both systems is similar. In fact, with the greed factor, the two economies have a flatter curve than that of Figure 5.3 when exchange rate equals 1. Opportunistic breach of faith seems to actually benefit the economies by creating a large middle class with a higher average purchasing power. Perhaps, this is how the common belief has developed that greed and opportunism creates a free market, since when everybody is opportunistic the ill effects of opportunism cancel each other out and people don't have to be stuck with non-performing commitments. This is true only as long as there are no arbitrage related economic skews.

When the exchange rate increases even a little more than the PPP rate, we see that the weaker system ends up with a far lesser purchasing power than the stronger one. This is so much so that, when the exchange rate is 30 or 50, we hardly see the dash line in the figure. In addition, as the exchange rate increases, the solid line becomes vertical much faster than its counterparts from Figure 5.3. The average purchasing power in the stronger system is also much lower when exchange rate is 50 (around 1,000), than when it is 1 (around 5,000). The weak system not only suffers from a vastly diminished purchasing power, the stronger system also becomes increasingly polarized and its average purchasing power reduces.

How do we explain this behaviour? Consider the different kinds of links that exist in this system. They can be labelled as "s → s", "s → w", "w → s" and "w → w". These denote links from strong to strong, strong to weak, weak to strong and weak to weak nodes, respectively. When opportunism sets in, which links are most likely to break? We can see that s → w and w → w links are most vulnerable in that order. Wealth coming from a w node gets *divided* by the exchange rate if it is paid to a s node and wealth coming from a s node gets *multiplied* if it is paid to a w node. In either case, an incoming link to a w node has the highest probability to be thrown away. This brings down the buying power of w nodes drastically. Not only are people in the stronger system unwilling to meet demands in the weaker system, but even neighbours within the weaker system are as unwilling to meet the demands of one another.

On the other hand, links going from the weaker system to the stronger system are more likely to persist. Since these links also behave in an opportunistic manner, they eventually tend to connect to wealthier nodes, giving them more purchasing power. Sensitivity to initial conditions set in, and small initial differences accentuate making the system more polarized.

In reality, global markets are somewhere between the systems portrayed in Figures 5.3 and 5.4. First, we are yet to become a completely connected world. In the simulations, anyone could do business with anyone else in the two systems. But in reality, this is not so and there are still intermediaries while doing business. This is especially true when trade has to happen across linguistic boundaries and vastly different cultural groups.

Second, the extent of opportunistic breach of trust depends on a number of things like local culture, personal values and the kind of business transaction involved. It is somewhat more common to witness opportunistic leaps in industries like retailing consumer goods. However, in business relationships involving large-scale contracts like construction of airports or roads, or even in maintenance of critical business software, business relationships cannot be cancelled so easily by either party.

Third, the kind of global trade modelled in the simulation holds good only when there is no physical movement of materials involved. If a business transaction requires working with material goods, then it is more likely to see a clustered graph with business transactions happening only when the cost of material movement is low. On the other hand, if we consider industries like software, publishing, BPO units, call centres and so on, which do not require exchange of material, then the simulated model would be more accurate.

5.5 Regulate What: Material or Money?

One thing evident from the simulations is that a global free market is sustainable only when currency exchange rates converge to their PPP values. It is not only beneficial for the "weaker" system by giving it its correct purchasing power globally; it is also beneficial for stronger economies by preventing them from becoming polarized and in maintaining their free market competitiveness.

Given these, one of the pertinent questions to ask would be: what kinds of structural adjustments are necessary in order to make market driven exchange rates approach their PPP values? Independent, autonomous free-market decisions by individuals do not by themselves ensure global convergence towards PPP.

If this problem is not tackled with the urgency it deserves, we may see increased instances of tirades against globalization, and specifically arguments glorifying isolationism, paranoia and xenophobia. However, an incorrect way of addressing this problem would be to curb free trade altogether and position exchange rates artificially. This does not ensure in any way that exchange rates reflect relative purchasing power. It only serves to stifle free trade and to bring down the overall purchasing power.

As we become increasingly connected, we need to welcome new ideas, products and services from all over the world, without individuals losing their purchasing power in the process. However, we see that due to historical reasons, international trade today is configured to facilitate almost the exact opposite.

Import of goods from overseas are restricted by imposing import duties and the movements of people are restricted by stringent visa norms. However, there is a growing tendency towards removing restrictions on foreign money flowing into the economy.

We should keep restrictions on goods and people to the extent that illegal and harmful goods and persons do not enter the country. However, if import duty is levied to discourage foreign products from entering the country it just places an extra hurdle on foreign investors vying to meet demands of the indigenous population. If this is coupled with unrestricted foreign capital inflow into the system, all that it serves is to give the investors an opportunity to exploit arbitrage. For a foreign investor, meeting demands of this country by offering goods and services becomes less lucrative than having his own demands met, or meeting the demands in his own country by sourcing material and labour and issuing receipts (money) in return. When a number of people adopt this strategy, the redemption value of the receipts would plummet and local demands won't be met anyway.

Perhaps, we should be looking at the opposite configuration. If the movement of goods and people are made easier, and a cap is placed on capital inflow, then the main incentive for tapping a market would be to meet demands of the local population rather than entice them with "money". Investors would also find it cheaper to set up production and manufacturing units locally rather than *import* finished goods. This helps not only in generating more employment but also in strengthening the local "capability". Currently, while enormous employment is being generated, the average buying power is still very low. At least, it is not growing at the pace that employment is being generated.

Some examples may make the argument clear. A few years ago in India, imported technical books for engineering were enormously expensive. The currency conversion rates, coupled with import duty, made them unaffordable for a large proportion of the population. However, lately, there is a shift towards printing "low-priced editions" of these books. Typically, the books are sent as a soft copy over the Internet to a publishing unit inside India. It is not feasible to impose "import duty" on an e-mail that enters the country. When such books are published locally, the costs of publishing are much lower (with the market conversion rate), which helps the publisher to offer books at a much lower price within India. The result of this is that Indian consumers now have a larger palette of books as their options. It does not matter if I don't have Rs 5,000 to buy a particular book if the same book is printed locally and offered at Rs 500. Having a budget of Rs 1,000 for buying would still have made me poor as far as affording this book is concerned, had the book not been printed locally. The purchasing power of

Rs 500 is now worth the same as what Rs 5,000 was earlier, as far as this book is concerned.

There are also other examples of foreign automobile manufacturers collaborating with Indian counterparts to enter the Indian market. This collaboration was necessary since foreign direct investment was not allowed during that time (late 1980s). However, the fallout of this was that several Indian automobile manufacturers are now capable of producing world-class automobiles by themselves. If the movement of materials and people were to have been easier, we may have perhaps witnessed a much better and more sustained growth.

But this argument begs the question: why should we restrict the inflow of either goods or money? Why not remove restrictions on the flow of both goods and money? In the simulation runs of Figures 5.3 and 5.4, restriction on flow of goods was not considered. Despite this, we see that disparities in exchange rates can lead to a highly skewed purchasing power distribution. The reason is that, when money inflow is not regulated, there is always an incentive to obtain greater "wealth" by arbitrage, rather than by meeting the demands of one another within the system. This weans the system away from any incentives for people to organize. Organization into groups, communities and institutions are essential for solving problems at a larger scale. Given the disincentive to organize, the result is simply a lowered overall purchasing power.

Notes

1. Monetary episodes from history. http://www.galmarley.com/framesets/fs_monetary_history_faqs.htm. Last accessed: 8 March 2006.

2. The Gold Rush home page by PBS: http://www.pbs.org/goldrush/. Last accessed: 8 March 2006.
3. Wikipedia article on the gold standard: http://www.en.wikipedia.org/wiki/Gold_standard. Last accessed: 8 March 2006.
4. Wikipedia article on the Irish potato famine: http://www.en.wikipedia.org/wiki/Irish_Potato_Famine. Last accessed: 8 March 2006.
5. Source: "Hard currency" page on Wikipedia: http://www.en.wikipedia.org/wiki/Hard_currency. Last accessed: 10 March 2006.

Chapter 6

Concluding Remarks

*[T]omorrow's development strategies will not come from
Washington or Paris, but will come from Latin America or
deep in Africa. They will be indigenous, matched to actual
local needs. They will not stress economics at the expense of
ecology, culture and other dimensions of existence. They will,
yet, reduce infant mortality, increase lifespan, nutrition, and
the general quality of life without giving up their core social
values or religion and without necessarily taking to Pepsi and
Pizzas that is part of the industrial civilization that is just 200
years old and has yet managed to wreck havoc on a scale
that has threatened the earth's vitals that has survived 60,000
years or 800 generations of the human species.*

—Alvin Toffler

In a concluding note, I would like to give some perspectives
on the road ahead, from a "developing" or Third World perspective. I don't like either of these terms and prefer to use
the term "non-industrialized" instead. Specifically, I don't think

the Third World can ever become "developed" in the conventional sense of the term that places such a huge burden on earth's perishable resources.

Currently, the industrialized world constitutes about a sixth of the total population of the world. There simply isn't enough resources on this earth to support a five times increase on the demands on them if the entire world becomes industrialized—in the form that industrialization is presently in.

Most of the countries that are categorized as non-industrialized today lie in parts of the world that are rich with natural resources and diversity of life forms. Historically, fighting against elements of nature was not a major challenge and resources for survival were available in plenty. In contrast, the industrial civilization that continues to impact us today was primarily driven by Western Europe and North America. In these areas, technology is more often a survival mechanism. Without technologies for heating, communication, transport and so on, several parts of Western Europe or North America would simply die of cold weather!

Industrial technology that is centred on mass production and standardization was not crucial for survival in India, Africa and Central America. Nothing attracts emphasis like survival; and since survival was not a major issue, most technical ideas generated in these places encountered societal inertia and died down much before making large-scale impacts.

Historically, in India, several technical innovations were developed and applied locally. The biggest challenges that Indian society faced (other than occasional wars, famines, etc.) were social in nature. This led to enormous explorations into our "inner" selves, probing the human body, behaviour, the nature of interpersonal relationships, the consciousness, and so on. In addition, several areas like mathematics, astronomy, medicine, yoga, architecture, city planning and even administrative concepts like democracy had developed to high levels of sophistication at different points in time at different places.

However, a dearth of technologies that can efficiently transport or even communicate across long distances ensured that the overall diameter of the society graph was high. The average length of the shortest path between any two arbitrarily chosen people involved a significant number of intermediaries.

Consequently, there are two prominent characteristics about collective knowledge in India and perhaps in many other non-industrialized countries. These are: diversity in standards with no single homogenous standard, and an enormous amount of communication distortion due to intermediaries.

However, a system with enormous diversity of ideas can be seen as diversity in the set of "memes". When these memes are connected by today's ICT, we are far more likely to see an explosion of different ideas evolving from this system. With the vast amount of misrepresentation also being present in the system, there are likely to be a number of conflicts of ideas. The main challenge would be to manage these conflicts such that they result in the evolution of better ideas and not let it degenerate into clashes.

We already see a number of examples of this phenomenon in action. The number of debates and talk shows on television channels has grown enormously in the recent years. In addition, there is a vast and growing pool of bloggers debating almost every pertinent issue over blogs. There have also been episodes of conflict and an assertion of rights to free speech on these blogs.

Similarly, my conjecture is that ICT is primarily responsible for the sudden emergence of several "sparks" in different areas such as sports, science, technology and the arts. Over

the recent years, there has been an increase in the number of young achievers in what were previously unconventional areas like Tennis and Formula One racing. Similarly, there seems to be a number of silent revolutions in building energy efficient machines and buildings. People have been experimenting with natural gas and even vegetable oils to run automobiles and generators and harnessing solar power, wind power and rainwater for homes.

It is somewhat unfortunate that there are not many systematic studies exploring the changes in people's outlook and behaviour due to the penetration of ICT. There is a pressing need for modelling this vast idea pool and effectively harvesting ideas. At least, I don't know of any studies in India that have looked into the issue of ICT penetration from a *strategic* perspective—as a problem of harvesting ideas.

Generally such studies were not feasible, given the enormous complexity of social connections in India. But with rapid advances in high-performance computing, social information networks are a ripe area for exploration.

Bibliography and Selected Reading

Abiteboul, Serge, Preda, Mihai and Cobena, Gregory, 'Adaptive on-line page importance computation. In Proceedings of World Wide Web Conference 2003 (WWW2003), Budapest, Hungary, May 2003.

Adamic, L. A., *Zipf, Power-laws and Pareto: A ranking tutorial.* HP Information Dynamics Lab report, 2000. http://www.hpl.hp.com/research/idl/papers/ranking/ranking.html

Adamic, L. A. and Adar, E., 'You are what you link'. Proceedings of the 10th International World Wide Web Conference, Hong Kong, May 2001.

Adamic, L. A., Lukose, R., Puniyani, A. and Huberman, B., 'Search in power-law networks'. *Physical Review, E 64*, 046135, 2001.

Agre, Philip E., 'The market logic of information'. *Knowledge, Technology, and Policy, 13*(1): 67–77, 2001.

Albert, R., Jeong, H. and Barabasi, A., 'Diameter of the World Wide Web'. *Nature, 401*(September):130–31, 1999.

Axelrod, R., *The Evolution of Cooperation.* New York: Basic Books. 1985.

Barabási, Albert-László, *Linked: The new science of networks.* Perseus Books, 2002.

Barabási, Albert-László and Albert, Réka, 'Emergence of Scaling in Random Networks'. *Science, 206*:509, 1999.

Brin, S. and Page, L., 'The Anatomy of a Large-Scale Hypertextual Web Search Engine', Proceedings of WWW7, May 1998, 107–17.

Broeder, A., Kumar, R., Maghoul, F., Raghavan, P., Rajagopalan, S., Stata, R., Tomkins, A. and Wiener, J., 'Graph Structure in the Web'. In Proc. 9th WWW Conference, Amsterdam, 2000.

Brooks, Rodney A., *Cambrian Intelligence: The Early History of the New AI*. Cambridge, Massachusetts: MIT Press, 1999.

Camerer, Colin., 'Bounded Rationality in Individual Decision Making'. Working Papers 1029, California Institute of Technology, Division of the Humanities and Social Sciences. 1998.

Davies, Glyn, *A History of money from ancient times to the present day*, 3rd. ed. Cardiff: University of Wales Press, 2002.

Dawkins, Richard, *The Selfish Gene*. NY: Oxford University Press, 2nd edn, 1989.

Dillman, Don A., *Mail and Internet Surveys: A Tailored Design Method*. New York: John Wiley & Sons, 1999.

Elmacioglu, E. and Lee, D., 'On Six Degrees of Separation in DBLP-DB and More'. *ACM SIGMOD Record, 34* (2): 33–40, 2005.

Erdös, P. and Rényi, A., 'On random graphs'. *Publ. Math. Debrecen, 6*: 290–97, 1959.

Faloutsos, M., Faloutsos, P. and Faloutsos, C., 'On Power-Law Relationships of the Internet Topology.' Proceedings of ACM SIGCOMM '99, 251–62.

Gladwell, Malcolm, *The Tipping Point: How little things can make a big difference*. UK: Little, Brown, 2002.

Gleick, James, *Chaos: Making a New Science*. Penguin (Non-classics), 1998.

Goldhaber, Michael, 'The Attention Economy and the Net'. First-Monday: Peer-reviewed journal on the Internet. Vol 2, No. 4, 1997. http://www.firstmonday.dk/issues/issue2_4/goldhaber/

Goyal, Ashima, 'Foreign Inflows: Evil, Blessing or Opportunity?' In K. S. Parikh (ed.), *Mid-Year review of the Indian economy, 1994–95*, New Delhi: Konark Publishers, 1995.

Hardin, Garrett, 'The Tragedy of the Commons'. *Science, 162*: 1243–48, 1968.

Hayes, Brian, 'Graph theory in practice—Part I'. *American Scientist, 88* (1): 9–13, 2000.

———, 'Graph theory in practice—Part II'. *American Scientist, 88* (2): 104–109, 2000.

Judge, Joseph, 'The Travail of Ireland'. *National Geographic, 159* (4): 432–40, 1981.

Kahneman, D. and Tversky, A., 'The psychology of preferences'. *Scientific American, 246* (1): 160–73, 1982.

Keeling, M., 'The mathematics of diseases'. *Plus Magazine,* March 2001. http://www.plus.maths.org/issue14/features/diseases/index-gifd.html

Kleinberg, J., 'The small-world phenomenon: An algorithmic perspective'. 2000. http://www.cs.cornell.edu/home/kleinber/swn.ps

Kuhn, Thomas S., *The structure of scientific revolutions,* 3rd ed. Chicago: University of Chicago Press, 1996.

Li, T. Y. and Yorke, J. A., 'Period Three Implies Chaos'. *American Math. Monthly, 82:* 985–92, 1975.

Lyman, Peter and Varian, Hal R., 'How Much Information, 2003'. SIMS Technical Report. Retrieved from http://www.sims.berkeley.edu/how-much-info-2003 April 2005.

Malhotra, R., 'The Peer Review Cartel'. *Outlook India,* February 2004.

Mandelbrot, B. and Hudson, R.L., *The (Mis) Behavior of Markets.* New York: Basic Books, 2004.

Markie, Peter, 'Rationalism vs. Empiricism'. In Edward N. Zalta (ed.), *The Stanford Encyclopedia of Philosophy* (Fall 2004 Edition), http://www.plato.stanford.edu/archives/fall2004/entries/rationalism-empiricism/

Marschak, J., 'Elements for a Theory of Teams'. Cowles Commission, University of Chicago, 1955.

Mayer, C., 'The Riddle of the Nile'. *Kitco Exclusive Commentaries,* March 2005. http://www.kitco.com/ind/Mayer/mar142005.html. Last accessed: 10 March 2006.

Mehta, Pratap Bhanu, 'Lessons on Globalisation from India'. *YaleGlobal,* June 2004.

Milgram, Stanley, 'The Small World Problem'. *Psychology Today,* May 1967.

Mises, Ludwig von, *'The theory of money and credit'.* First published 1912. Translated from German by H. E. Batson. Liberty Fund, Indianapolis, 1981.

Moffatt, Mike, 'A beginners guide to purchasing power parity (PPP) theory'. http://www.economics.about.com/cs/money/a/purchasingpower.htm

———, 'What is arbitrage? About.com Economics article'. http://www.economics.about.com/cs/finance/a/arbitrage.htm. Last accessed: 10 March 2006.

Newman, M. E. J. , Watts, D. J. and Strogatz, S. H., 'Random graph models of social networks'. Proceedings of the National Academy of Sciences, USA, Vol. 99, No. 1, February 2002.

Ramya, N. and Srinivasa, Srinath, 'How does ICT influence decision-making: An empirical study'. Technical Report, International Institute of Information Technology, Bangalore (IIIT-B), December 2005.

Raymond, Eric S., *The Cathedral and the Bazaar*. Cambridge: O'Reilly, 2001.

———, 'The Magic Cauldron'. Thyrsus Enterprises. http://www.tuxedo.org/~esr/. Last accessed: 9 February 2006.

Rogers, Everett M., 'The diffusion of innovations', 4th ed. New York: Free Press, 1995.

Sen, Amartya, *Poverty and Famines: An Essay on Entitlements and Deprivation*. Oxford: Clarendon Press, 1982a.

———, *Choice, Welfare and Measurement*. Oxford: Basil Blackwell, 1982b.

———, *The Argumentative Indian: Writings on Indian History, Culture and Identity*. London: Allen Lane, 2005.

Senge, Peter M., 'The Fifth Discipline', 1st ed. New York: Currency, 1994.

Seth, Kiran, 'Our core competence. SPIC MACAY article head'. http://www.spicmacay.com/article_view.as?articleid=0. Last accessed: 10 March 2006.

Simon, Herbert A., 'A Behavioral Model of Rational Choice', *Quarterly Journal of Economics*, Vol. 69, pp. 99–108, 1955.

———, 'The Logic of Rational Decision. Complex Information'. Processing Paper #74. Carnegie Institute of Technology. 1964.

———, *Theories of Bounded Rationality: Decision and Organization*, pp. 161–76. Amsterdam: North-Holland Publishing Company, 1972.

Smyth, Jolene D., Dillman, Don A., Christian, Leah Melani and Stern, Michael J., 'How Visual Grouping Influences Answers to Internet Surveys'. American Association for Public Opinion Research Meetings, May 2004.

Strogatz, S. H., 'Exploring complex networks'. *Nature*, 410: 268–76, 2001.

———, *Sync: The emerging science of spontaneous order*. New York: Theia, 2003.

Toffler, Alvin, *Future Shock*. New York: Bantam Books. 1970.

———, *The Third Wave*. New York: Bantam Books, 1980.

———, *Powershift: Knowledge, Wealth and Violence at the Edge of the 21st Century*. New York: Bantam Books, 1990.

Watts, Duncan J., 'A simple model of global cascades on random networks'. Proceedings of the National Academy of Sciences, USA, Vol. 99, No. 9, 2002.

———, *Six Degrees: The Science of a Connected Age*. London: William Heinemann, 2003.

Watts, Duncan and Strogatz, Steve, 'Collective Dynamics of Small-World Networks'. *Nature, Vol. 393*, 4 June 1998.

Weisstein, Eric W., 'Self-Similarity. From MathWorld—A Wolfram Web Resource', 1999. http://www.mathworld.wolfram.com/Self-Similarity.html.

Weisstein, Eric W. and Tony Weisstan, 'Kermack-McKendrick Model'. From *MathWorld*—A Wolfram Web Resource, 2004. http://www.mathworld.wolfram.com/Kermack-McKendrickModel.html.

World Bank, 'Data by topic: GDP (PPP)'. http://www.worldbank.org/data/databytopic/GDP_PPP.pdf, 2005.

Index